D0508205

BK54812

# illustration
# pocket essentials

**ILLUSTRATION POCKET ESSENTIALS**
First published in the United Kingdom in 2010 by
I L E X
210 High Street
Lewes
East Sussex BN7 2NS
www.ilex-press.com

Text © Steve Caplin and Adam Banks 2002
Design and layout © 2010 The Ilex Press Limited

Publisher: Alastair Campbell
Creative Director: Peter Bridgewater
Managing Editor: Nick Jones
Editor: Ellie Wilson
Art Director: Julie Weir
Designer: Graham Davis

British Library Cataloguing-in-Publication Data
A catalogue record for this book is available from
the British Library

ISBN: 978-1-907579-04-2

10 9 8 7 6 5 4 3 2 1

Printed in China

Colour Origination by Ivy Press Reprographics.

# ◼ Introduction

# ◼ The basics

# ◼ Digital painting

# ◼ Digital drawing

# ◼ 3D illustration

# ◼ Animation

# ◼ Artist at work

# ◼ Reference

# introduction

This book is about a revolution, and how to join it.

Once, computer-generated art was not much more than a collection of slick, machine-made images. They were images that lacked any human interest, where everything looked pretty much the same; it was the only look that the available programs could produce. At first the novelty of this new form of image making was intriguing, but it wasn't long before it soured into cliché. When I saw my twentieth checkerboard grid stretching far away into the Dali-like landscape, reflecting the realistic clouds floating above it, I was sure that this medium was stuck in some kind of art hole where imagination doesn't get much play.

But the fascination with easy effects went away as the technology grew up. Technology started to listen to artists and designers; it invited them into software development discussions alongside the engineers and programmers who had previously held sway over what a computer application of this sort could do. In time, artists passed into a second era of digital image making: we made computers do what we wanted them to do, not what programmers suggested we do.

Now we've progressed to another stage of digital illustration: an era that I would not have thought possible those few years back at the clichéd dawn. This one is a revolution. Throughout history, advances in technology have made complicated tasks easier to do, and in some cases they have enabled whole new areas of art to exist. Before the late 19th century, artists could make sketches outside, but needed to return to their studios to paint. The reason was very basic—the amount of paint needed for a day's work would dry up in the open air. This all changed with the simple invention of small metal tubes to hold the artists' colors: a seemingly insignificant advance, but one that enabled the early Impressionists to go outdoors to complete whole canvases. The change of tools was simple, but the effects changed the face of modern art.

Now computers, often derided as no more than a clever tool—especially in the context of art and design—are giving artists and designers actual ideas as well as new ways to draw them. That's a very different order of change from the way painting changed back in the 1870s.

Many of us have clung fiercely to the notion that the content of an illustration, diagram, painting, or animation is the most important part of it, and that the way the content gets onto paper, electrons, or film is secondary. Craft is good, and style is good, and balance and aesthetics are good, but they pale next to the idea behind the work. I think that we're finding out that a "mere tool" is making more of a contribution than we thought, and that there's some rethinking to do—and some respect to dole out, too.

Why do we want to create images that are, say, indistinguishable from photographs? The documentary nature of photography—the idea that the camera never lies—was debunked long before digital manipulation was possible. The techniques of manipulation were clumsier, but they still existed. From cave painting on, image making has followed technological advances and will continue to do so. Digital illustration is a way to make pictures. But this time technology does more than simply enable the artist to create startling, funny, informative, beautiful images. This time the power of computing itself—the speed of the machine together with the sophistication of the software—is making more than a "mere tool" contribution.

This book will take you on a learning journey into this revolutionary new world. Here is a clearly delineated, step-by-step look at every aspect of digital illustration and how it's done. Digital painting, drawing, 3D illustration, and animation are examined and showcased with amazing examples. Many of these images were unachievable, would have been unthinkable, before the new revolution.

# THE BASICS

ILLUSTRATION METHODS
WHAT YOU'LL NEED

**ESSENTIAL EQUIPMENT** Buying your first computer, or choosing the best software and applications for an existing one, can be a daunting task. But it does not need to be.

# WHAT YOU'LL NEED

Whether you opt for a PC or an Apple Macintosh, there's no need to understand all of the jargon; a basic comprehension of the hardware and the demands of digital imaging will suffice. The same goes for buying a scanner, printer, or digital camera. It doesn't get any more complicated when you come to choosing software. If you already know what you are trying to achieve, the information in this chapter should point you toward the right application for the job. If not, then you should get a few good ideas. Above all, there is no need to spend huge amounts of money on digital illustration—though if you have the cash to spare then there is plenty of opportunity to do so!

Buying a computer is your first step into digital illustration. Current models fall into two categories: PC or Apple Macintosh. They have similar capabilities, but inherent technical differences limit the choice of software and add-ons.

Macs are the standard choice for professional graphics users, having been developed with this task in mind; you will see them in most design studios, advertising agencies, and publishing houses. However, they are less popular as general-purpose machines, as they tend to be slightly more expensive than PCs and offer a smaller choice of office and leisure software. On the other hand, PCs can be more difficult to use and maintain, partly because they are governed by complex standards and built by many different manufacturers. Macs are made by only one company, Apple, which can therefore manage their specifications in a more straightforward manner.

The essential components of any computer include a processor, memory, a hard disk, and an operating system. The processor is the brain of the machine—while you are working, there will often be short delays as the computer catches up with what you are asking it to do, or "process"; a faster processor means less waiting. Computer adverts

Opposite: Mouse for an Apple Macintosh computer; Macs have played a central role in the development of professional computer graphics, both in print and multimedia/online.

# What you'll need

often quote processor speed, which is measured in gigahertz (GHz), as an indicator of performance, but it is not a comprehensive arbiter. Older Macs had Motorola G4 and G5 processors. Now that all Macs use Intel processors it is possible to make direct technical speed comparisons—although this is just one aspect.

Overall speed is also affected by other components in the computer system. The graphics card, which helps drive the screen display, is a prime example, particularly when it comes to intensive 3D work. Look at reviews in computer magazines for more meaningful performance ratings of different models.

While you are using a particular piece of software, or "application," such as Adobe Photoshop, both the application and the data it is working on—for example, your illustration—are stored in the computer's memory. This consists of banks of silicon chips, and is known as "random access" memory (RAM) because the processor can quickly get information in or out of any part of it at any time. When the computer is turned off, however, everything in RAM is lost. So applications and data are stored permanently on a sealed mechanical device, called the hard disk. This is why you must remember to save work at regular intervals, which is the process of copying it from RAM to the hard disk.

Memory and hard disk capacities are measured in bytes. One megabyte (1 MB) equals just over a million bytes, while a gigabyte (1 GB) is a thousand times as much again. For basic work, you will need at least 1GB of RAM: around 4 GB is sensible for serious Photoshop and 3D work. Hard disks start at around 100 GB, but for serious 3D and animation work, you are likely to use many hundreds of gigabytes.

Always be aware that hard disks can fail. This does not happen too often, but it makes sense to keep a back-up copy of important data on a separate storage media, such as recordable CDs or external hard drives. Any work that is not in regular use can also be "archived" onto such media, removing it from the hard disk and therefore making room for new files.

The operating system is a piece of "permanent" software that is loaded from the hard disk whenever the computer is turned on, and is basically the platform on which all applications run. One of the operating system's main functions is to manage memory, so that several applications can run at once and share the available RAM. It can also make extra space available by swapping data temporarily to the hard disk, which is known as "virtual memory" (some applications also swap data independently between RAM and their own area of the hard disk, known as a "scratch disk").

PCs generally use the Windows operating system, developed by Microsoft, the latest version of which is Windows 7. Macs use the Mac OS X, created by Apple. You can only run applications labeled for the particular operating system you use.

Although it is important to choose a suitable machine in the first place, components can be

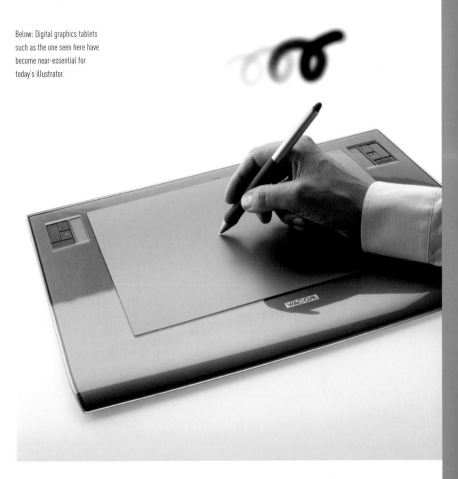

Below: Digital graphics tablets such as the one seen here have become near-essential for today's illustrator.

added later. Most computers are designed to be "opened up" by the user, and minor upgrades should not invalidate the warranty. In PCs, processors and graphics cards can often be replaced, but in any computer a memory upgrade is usually more effective. RAM chips, usually known as "DIMMs," fit easily into slots inside the computer. If no slots are free, then you will have to remove an existing DIMM to add a larger one.

**THE SCREEN** is arguably one of the most important pieces of equipment the digital illustrator will use. Screen size, resolution, and clarity can have a significant effect on the quality of not just your artwork, but also your working life. So getting the right one is important. With traditional media, your artwork is always in front of you. You can look at any part of it, tilt it, or get close up for fine detail. Using a computer is quite different.

# Monitors

When your illustration is displayed on-screen at actual size, the level of detail visible is actually quite coarse. For close work, you will need to "zoom in" and show a small area at high magnification. This is one reason why, when it comes to monitors, bigger is better.

When you zoom in to, say, 200%, you are quadrupling the space you would need to keep the whole illustration in the monitor's view. Areas outside the screen can be seen by clicking scroll bars, which basically "slide" the artwork around. The larger your display, the less time you will spend zooming in and out and scrolling around your artwork.

A second demand on screen space comes from the software. To access all the commands and controls in your painting and drawing applications, you are provided with various toolbars and palettes. These can be opened and closed as required, but it is more convenient to leave them open permanently. However, with a small monitor, they may take up more space than the artwork itself. The problem is even more acute with 3D and animation packages.

Gone are the days when you had to weigh up the differences between CRT monitors (the bulky cathode-ray tube variety) and LCD (liquid crystal display, found in today's flat screens); you'll only find LCD monitors offered with new systems. In deciding what monitor you prefer (and can afford), the major consideration is the size: 18 inches is a fair practical minimum for illustration work, 20 inches and above is quite common for desktop displays, with 27- and 30-inch screens as the highly-desirable but high-cost choices.

When looking at technical specifications there are different kinds of LCD technology to consider. TN screens are generally the cheapest, but they also tend to have a narrow practical viewing angle; looking from off to one side makes colours shift. IPS screens (as used in all iMacs today) are the high-end variety, and VA screens are the mid-point in price and quality. Remember that you'll be looking at this device for a very long time and relying on it absolutely for accurate color and clear display of your work, so don't compromise if you can possibly help it.

A few computers come with integral monitors, and here you will need to consider the pros and cons of the whole package. The best-known example is Apple's iMac, originally launched with a built-in CRT and later revamped with an LCD. Today's models come with 21.5- and 27-inch LCD screens of exceptionally high quality, so these are very good options.

How much you can see at any one time, however, depends not only on the physical size of the screen, but also on the resolution you set.

Resolution is measured in pixels, the colored dots generated by your computer to construct the screen image. The maximum resolution is dictated by the monitor, but most users will find it too high. This is because palettes, icons, and text labels are usually displayed at a fixed size, set in pixels.

As you increase resolution and pack more pixels into the same area, each pixel gets smaller, and items become less legible. Your artwork benefits, however, because you can zoom in to restore its physical size while seeing finer detail. Trial and error will find a resolution that balances these factors to suit your preference. LCDs have a fixed resolution, simulating smaller sizes by interpolation, which gives a noticeably less sharp image. You should avoid LCD monitors that cram a very high resolution into a smaller size (1920 x 1080 in a 17-inch screen, for example); you may find text hard to read, and

scaling things up to compensate for this will also soften them.

Finally, there is the question of proportion, or aspect ratio. Monitors used to be set to the traditional 4:3 ratio format, like older TVs, but many are now widescreen, using the 16:9 or slightly taller 16:10 ratio instead. This gives space for software tool palettes beside rather than on top of your work. For similar reasons, a number of users prefer to work across two monitors simultaneously, with palettes and toolbars on one and the image itself on the other. The downside of this is cost. Unless your graphics card supports a twin-monitor display, you may need a second graphics card as well as the extra screen.

Below: Apple's iMac computers come with integral monitors.

BEING ABLE to get things in and out of your computer is an essential requirement for the digital illustrator. Here, we look at some of the extras you may want to consider.

# Input and output

Much of the work of a digital illustrator can be generated wholly on a computer, but there are times when you need to import artwork from other sources. You will need a scanner of some sort if you want to get flat artwork into your computer, as well as a digital camera to capture real-life people, backgrounds, and objects. At some stage, you are also going to need to print out your work—most illustrations intended for publication can be emailed directly to the client, but there are times when a proof print is invaluable. Even if you never print a single image, you will still need a printer just to print out your invoices.

### SCANNERS

Scanners have come down in price tremendously over the last few years, and you can now pick up an entry-level model for less than $50 (£30). On the other hand, it is possible to spend a hundred times that on a high-end pre-press model. So what's the difference?

Essentially, the more expensive the scanner, the better the image quality. There is no need to spend too much, however. High-end scanners are required by professional publishers and repro houses in order to achieve perfect quality for print, but the needs of the illustrator are much less demanding. Usually, you will need a scanner only to scan in a rough sketch for use as a template in your favorite drawing or painting application. Even the cheapest flatbed scanner will be sufficient for this task.

If you need to scan transparencies, from 35mm slides to negatives to larger format images, there are two main options. The most cost-effective is to choose a flatbed scanner with a transparency adapter. In most cases this will be incorporated into the scanner lid, providing a light source that shines through the transparency onto the scanner head itself. The latest flatbed models, which can be picked up for as little as $250 (£150), offer sufficient resolution to magnify a 35mm slide to full-page size and beyond (although quality will be limited).

If you need to scan transparencies for positional or template purposes only, or if your work will involve substantial reworking of the scanned image, that option may be acceptable. However, if you need to scan for finished artwork, you might find that the output fails to measure up. If that is the case, you will need to invest in a dedicated slide scanner, which can cost anywhere from $700 (£450) upward. One low-cost alternative is a transparency adapter for a digital camera. Nikon, for example, makes an adapter that costs under $90 (£60), screws onto the lens mount of their cameras, and generates images as good as those that the camera can capture. You can also buy film scanners from around $150 (£100). While these are designed to handle 35mm and APS films, quality will vary and at the low end you might be better off with a decent flatbed. Remember, though, that digital cameras are now the norm; consider how many transparencies you'll really need to scan.

## CAMERAS

A digital camera is essential for the illustrator. The ability to capture people and objects instantaneously, with no running costs, makes them a must-have accessory. Digital cameras range in price from under $40 to several thousand dollars. Other than lens quality, the main difference is in the size of the image captured, which is measured in megapixels (millions of pixels). Good mid-range cameras can cost anywhere between $150 (£100) for a 10-megapixel version to around $500 (£320) for a 15-megapixel model.

## PRINTERS

There are two main kinds of printer: ink-jet and laser. Ink-jets produce the best quality pictures and, surprisingly, are the cheaper option. A $200 (£130) ink-jet printer, when used with a high-quality photographic paper, will create prints that are virtually indistinguishable from photographic prints. They are, however, slow—a U.S. Letter print can take several minutes. Ink-jets are also very expensive to run, with a single set of replacement cartridges, which last just a few hundred pages, costing up to $60 (£40).

It is mainly for reasons of speed that professional designers and publishers choose laser printers, even though their quality of reproduction is not as photographic as inkjets. A color laser printer of reasonable quality will cost a few hundred dollars at least, but running costs are just a few cents per page. Another reason for choosing a laser printer is that they tend to be PostScript devices. PostScript is the graphics language used by drawing programs. If you work in this field, you may find that you have to buy a software RIP (Raster Image Processor) to convert PostScript data into a form that ink-jet printers understand, or export PDFs and print those instead.

Below: Flatbed scanners such as this one are essential if you need to get physical, real-world artwork into your computer.

**1**

# ILLUSTRATION METHODS

**ILLUSTRATORS** working with traditional media are used to having a range of materials with which to work, and whichever they employ for a particular project will depend on their own skills, medium, preferences, and the requirements of the particular work in hand.

It is no different in the world of digital illustration. In fact, the range of tools and options available is bewildering. However, once you get past the barriers of terminology you will find that the different methods and applications break down into a handful of groups, and you are never restricted to just one. By understanding the basic concepts, then mixing and matching techniques, you can exploit the full potential of your art.

Opposite: Bitmap (paint) applications include photographic elements such as this lamp, which has been cut out from its background.

## BITMAP VS. VECTOR VS. 3D

Digital illustration falls into three main categories: bitmap (also known as "painting"), vector (also known as "drawing"), and 3D modeling. Although the end results can often look similar, they are three very different disciplines, and the professional digital artist needs to be adept at working in all three styles.

## BITMAP ILLUSTRATION (PAINTING)

A bitmap is an image that has been broken down into a regular array of tiny squares, known as pixels. Each pixel may be one of over 16 million different colors, and for illustration purposes the pixels are generally so small that you see the final image as a continuous tone, rather than as a grid of squares. With painting applications, you create marks on the screen just as if you were painting on paper or canvas. Modern painting applications provide multiple layers, which can be used for different elements in your illustration, rather like painting on several sheets of glass overlaid on each other; each layer can be moved, scaled, colored, and distorted independently of the others.

Popular painting applications include Adobe Photoshop, Corel Painter, and Corel PaintShop Photo Pro.

# Illustration methods

## VECTOR ILLUSTRATION (DRAWING)

Vector programs use a mathematical graphics language to define individual shapes. As well as drawing basic rectangles, ellipses, and polygons, vector applications can create smooth curves, known as Bézier curves, which enable the artist to draw any shape imaginable.

In drawing applications, each element of the illustration is a separate object. This differs from the layers model in painting applications, where an image of a telephone, say, may be on a different layer to the desk on which it stands.

In a drawing application, each constituent part of the telephone—the outline of the tele-phone, the receiver, the shapes of the buttons, the numbers on the buttons, and so on—will be a distinct element. In a way, it is a little like working with a large number of individual pieces of paper, each of which can be reshaped or re-colored at will.

The popular vector, or drawing, applications include Adobe Illustrator and CorelDRAW.

## 3D MODELING

Whereas both vector and bitmap illustration involve drawing or painting artwork in a manner familiar to even the most traditional of artists, 3D modeling is a very different discipline. In most 3D applications, objects are created by extruding or revolving drawn outlines—in the most basic sense, it is like spinning a curve around a lathe axis to create a solid object.

On top of that, the more sophisticated 3D modeling programs offer a huge range of further distortion and modeling techniques, which can enable skilled users to create a variety of forms.

Far left: Once the image has been digitized, it is possible to apply a wide range of effects to it, such as this Pointillist filter.

Left: The cutout object can be placed on another background—here, shading and a bright spot for the bulb have been added.

Left: Vector (draw) applications treat each element as a separate object. This drawing has been traced over the original lamp.

Above and right: The lamp is generated in a 3D application by drawing its outline in 2D and spinning it around a central axis. The lathe process results in a wireframe model, which describes the lamp as a three-dimensional object. Shading, texture, and color can be assigned to each individual element. Here, the focal length of the virtual camera has been changed to add perspective.

Right: Some vector applications let the user apply natural-looking brush strokes to the outline, and also add detailed shading.

Unlike painting or drawing applications, 3D modelers create "solid" objects that can be manipulated within a virtual environment. Different textures can be applied to the surface —you can set it up to suggest a light is shining on it, for example—and the surface itself can be spun around and viewed from any angle. This may be a laborious process, but the object can serve a wide range of purposes once modeled.

Popular 3D applications range from simple dedicated programs like Corel Bryce and Poser to high-end modelers, such as NewTek's LightWave and Autodesk's Maya.

## ANIMATION

Computer animations can be based on any of the three disciplines outlined above, using a "timeline" that lets elements vary in position and size over time. Animation programs produce movies as their finished product, which can then be sent for TV broadcast, distributed on CDs or DVDs, or—at lower resolution—shown on the Internet. Typical animation applications include Adobe Flash, Adobe After Effects, and Toon Boom Studio.

**PAINTING DIGITALLY** is a very different proposition to the traditional method of using a brush and canvas. Resolution, pixels, masking, and style all need to be considered. Bitmap images, as we have said previously (page 18), consist of a grid of pixels, each with its own color value.

# Painting

When you first create a new document in a bitmap application, such as Adobe Photoshop, it is empty; all the pixels are set to one color, normally white. You can then use brush tools to apply color to this blank canvas by changing the values of the pixels under the cursor. If you open up a digitized photo, you will see an image that is made up of varying color values. You can also apply adjustments and filters to all the pixels at once, changing the color of the whole image.

These two ways of manipulating bitmaps—painting directly onto them, and making global adjustments using numbers and sliders—provide the basic capabilities you need to alter images. Two important additional elements, however, are masks and layers. Masks (as in conventional disciplines such as acrylic and airbrush) enable you to restrict changes to certain parts of your artwork, leaving others intact. Layers, on the other hand, enable you to create and manipulate different elements of an illustration independently, arranging them above and below each other within the visible canvas. We will explore these facilities further in Part 3.

The number of pixels that make up an image determines its resolution. To fool your eye into believing that it is seeing a complete picture, rather than a grid of colored squares, there must be enough pixels packed into a given area. On the computer screen, where the monitor's glow helps pixels blur together, about 72 pixels per inch—that is, a grid of 72 x 72 pixels in each

**Image Size**

Pixel Dimensions: 8.24M

Width: 1800 pixels
Height: 1200 pixels

OK
Cancel
Auto...

Document Size:

Width: 6 inches
Height: 4 inches
Resolution: 300 pixels/inch

☐ Scale Styles
☐ Constrain Proportions
☑ Resample Image:
Bicubic (best for smooth gradients)

When setting or checking the resolution of source material, do not forget to allow for cropping. This photo is a respectable 6 x 4 inches at 300 ppi, but when cropped to highlight a single object, it is reduced to a couple of inches. Photoshop tells us the image's pixel size, physical dimensions, and ppi; changing any of these will adjust the others to match. Alternatively, click Resample Image to change the actual pixel size by interpolating.

square inch of the image—is sufficient. If your illustration is for a website, you can simply make your image the required pixel size, and it will be the same on the end user's screen as on yours.

But things are not so straightforward if your work is destined for printing. On the page, you need upward of 200 pixels, or dots, per inch, with 300 being the typical value. When you start an illustration, it is vital to take this into account when setting the document's resolution. Too low, and your work will be ruined by a blocky appearance when printed. Too high is less problematic—resolution can be reduced—but large files will slow down your software, waste disk space, and take longer to email or transfer to storage media.

Resolution can be expressed either by a pixel count, such as "1,200 x 900," or by a combination of physical dimensions and pixels per inch (ppi), such as "4 x 3 inches at 300 ppi." Your software will accept the information in either form, and convert between them, which can be helpful when using existing material. You can also enter larger or smaller values and ask the software to re-sample the image to that size. This will be successful when scaling down, but scaling up is another matter, as the software has to interpolate extra pixels based on the color values of the existing ones, and the result is always slightly blurred.

The leading bitmap application, used both for manipulating photos and for painting from scratch, is Photoshop. Corel Photo-Paint is a solid alternative, while on the PC a number of good low-cost programs, such as Corel Paint Shop Pro, offer a more affordable entry point. A specialized area of painting is the simulation of natural media, including watercolors, oils, and inks. Photoshop has brushes that behave more like their real-world namesakes than conventional bitmap tools, but the concept is taken much further in Corel Painter, which simulates not only the initial effect of brush and pen strokes, but also the way paints and inks run together and into the surface of the paper.

The same image, reproduced at 300 ppi, 72 ppi, and 36 ppi (far left, left, and bottom left), shows progressively more visible pixellation. When the low-resolution copy is resampled up to the highest resolution using interpolation (bottom right), it loses much of its blockiness but does not regain the sharpness and detail of the original.

**DRAWING WITH A COMPUTER APPLICATION** can be a difficult technique to master, as it is far removed from its traditional process, and involves the manipulation of shapes and curves. However, mastery of the technique is essential for the digital illustrator. Drawing applications differ from painting applications in that you work with objects, rather than pixels.

# Drawing

Each object can be as basic as a circle or a rectangle, or a complex shape drawn with the Pen tool, which draws so-called Bézier curves—shapes devised by the French automotive designer Pierre Bézier in the 1960s. Each element of a curve is defined by four points: the starting and ending points, and two additional points that describe the shape and direction of the curve between its start and finish. You can read more about using Bézier curves on pages 74–77.

Each object created in a drawing application has two components: stroke and fill. The stroke is the outline around each "path," as the curves are known, and may be set to any color and thickness or given specific characteristics such as dotted lines and even arrowheads. Some applications, such as Illustrator, let the user wrap natural media and other brushstroke effects around stroked paths—see page 92 for more detail.

The fill element can be something as simple as defining a flat color for the interior of the object, to something more complex such as a gradient or pattern. One way of creating shading effects is to draw one path in a dark color and another, inside it, in a lighter version of the same color, and then create a blend between the two. This blend will take the form of a number of interpolated elements between the two initial objects, each being a step in both shape and color between the first and last. By increasing the number of steps, an effective impression of a smooth blend can be achieved.

Each object in a drawing program is a mathematically defined curve—although the illustrator needs to know nothing of the math behind it. The end effect is that each object can be re-colored and reshaped quickly and easily, with no loss of quality, because each object remains a discrete entity throughout the illustration process. In addition, artwork created using a drawing program can be resized as large as you like without any loss of quality—unlike the pixel method adopted by painting programs, the curve is simply redefined at a bigger size.

The Bézier curve method is a clever, mathematically efficient way of representing shapes and adjusting them, but it can be difficult to get the hang of. Perseverance pays off; they are the fundamental drawing tool, and their mastery is essential for any aspiring digital artist. Some programs make the task easier. Adobe Illustrator, for example, provides a Pencil tool that creates Bézier curves as you draw with the mouse or on a graphics tablet. These can then be reshaped simply by drawing over them, without having to use the Pen tool at all.

There are several drawing programs available, including CorelDraw and ACD Canvas, each of which has its own strengths. Canvas, for example, has a useful dimensioning feature that makes it invaluable for technical illustration. But in the professional arena, the only serious contender is Adobe Illustrator.

For the specialist illustration artist, Illustrator provides a solid working environment together with a custom brush technology that makes it hard to beat.

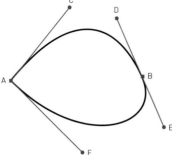

Above: In this simple path, points A and B are joined by curves. The shape of the curve from A to B is defined by the Bézier handles C and D: moving these will change the curve's shape. The lower curve, from B back to A, is defined by the handles E and F. The curve at point B is a smooth one, so the handle D to E forms a tangent to the curve at that point: where the two curves meet at point A, the handles C and F make a corner point.

Left: The stages in drawing simple artwork.
1. The outline of half the bottle is drawn using the Pen tool.
2. This outline is flipped across the vertical axis, and the two halves joined to make a single object.
3. The object's Fill is set to a dark green.
4. A smaller, brighter object is drawn inside the first to make the highlight.
5. The two elements are blended together to make a smooth transition from dark to light.
6. Other elements of the illustration are drawn as separate objects on top.

CREATING 3D MODELS can be a laborious and time-consuming task, but it can produce some dazzling results. Scenes and objects of surprising realism can be viewed from any angle and manipulated to your heart's content. 3D modeling is a unique way of generating illustrations: each element is built as a separate object by defining its profile on each of the three-dimensional planes.

# 3D modeling

Most modelers show the working view as either wireframe models or solid surfaces; in the latter case, these surfaces generally appear as if made of plastic to speed up the drawing process. Once the objects are modeled, they can have textures applied to them, giving them the appearance of wood, glass, metal, or any of thousands of different surfaces. The more complex modelers enable the user to tweak and adjust the settings for each surface in a variety of ways. For example, scanned artwork, showing both natural materials (wood, stone, and so on) and flat artwork (such as packaging illustrations), can be wrapped around the models as well.

Lighting adds not only highlights and shading, but also casts shadows on other objects in the scene. Most 3D applications enable the user to choose from a wide variety of light source types, which can be customized and moved at will.

Although building the original models can be a time-consuming task, the end result is a scene that can be viewed from any angle, comprising objects that can be endlessly manipulated and moved relative to each other. After a model has been built, the finished scene is "rendered"—that is, the finished artwork is generated complete with textures, reflections, and lighting effects. This process can take from a few minutes to several hours, depending on the complexity of the

models involved. For example, complex surfaces, such as glass and metals, will add significantly to the rendering time. A technique known as "ray tracing" calculates the way objects in the scene reflect and refract each other, producing a finished image of great realism.

3D modeling applications fall broadly into two categories: low end and high end. Low-end modelers include dedicated applications such as Corel Bryce (see page 134), which creates artificial landscapes using a wide variety of land, sky, and water elements. Bryce also enables the user to create and position primitive solids, such as cubes, spheres, and cylinders, within the scene. These can then be combined and textured to simulate such diverse things as spaceships, architecture, or many other kinds of objects.

Another low-end modeler is Poser (see page 138), which uses poseable human and animal models to create realistic figures that can be manipulated into any position.

High-end modelers, such as NewTek's LightWave and Autodesk's Maya (pages 140–155), require far more skill on the part of the user. Creating accurate and convincing models from scratch is a tricky task, but the results can be impressive. These are the kinds of modeling applications that are used to generate scenes and objects in high-budget films, and—with expertise—can create scenes that are indistinguishable from reality. As ever, the high-end/low-end divide is not absolute. Falling between the two are Adobe Illustrator, which uses basic modeling techniques to build simple objects, and DAZ Carrara, which combines the techniques of high-end modelers with a more approachable interface. The examples on these pages were created with Carrara.

Right: Professional 3D modeling programs typically use a window split four ways, to show the object or scene from the top, front, and side. The fourth pane normally shows the "camera" view, which can be moved and turned at will to show the object from any angle.

Far right: Each element of this trumpet has been modeled separately. This is the bell section, shown as a filled model; the "shadows" cast on the wall and floor describe the section's lathe profiles.

Right: This is the rendered model, after surface texture and reflection maps have been added. An image of this complexity would be almost impossible to draw by any other means.

ANIMATORS have always embraced a variety of media, and this continues in the digital domain. Any artwork—whether bitmap, vector, or 3D—can be turned into frame-by-frame animations. Illustrators are increasingly called upon to add the dimension of time to their work, whether delivering a finished product, as with web advertising banners, or contributing to a larger process, such as developing graphics for games or movies.

# Animation

The most widely commissioned form of animation at present is probably Flash. The name refers both to an application used to create animations, and to a widely supported format for delivering them via the Internet; both are owned by the graphics software company Adobe. Flash animations are vector-based, and use a simplified graphics language to store sequences in very small files. Bitmaps and video clips can be incorporated if necessary.

Because the format also offers interactivity, it's possible to build whole websites in Flash, with buttons and menus that respond to the user by changing the content that's displayed. More commonly, Flash is used for elements such as intro sequences and animated banners. Content will appear on users' screens only if they have a Flash plug in for their web browser software, but since the required download is available free of charge, this is very widely installed.

Flash owes some of its functionality to an earlier product, Adobe Director, which revolutionized multimedia design in the mid-1990s. The advent of CD-ROMs made it possible to distribute moving graphics and video for playback on PCs, and Director provided the tools to build these into interactive products. Its key feature was a timeline on which events could be arranged, and this persists as the basis of Flash

and other animation programs. Director is now used to create more advanced multimedia content in Adobe's Shockwave format, typically for CD-based training materials.

A more traditional approach to cartoon animation is facilitated by Toon Boom's Toon Boom Studio, which provides tools to draw objects, place them in a pseudo-3D scene, then animate them by moving both the objects themselves and the imaginary camera through which the scene is viewed. The results can be output as Flash files. The same company's Toon Boom Harmony covers more advanced projects.

Bitmap-based animation offers greater creative control, since there are no limits on what can be displayed. Images are imported into an application such as Adobe After Effects, where they can be arranged on a timeline and have adjustments, effects, and transitions applied. Extra features can be added via plug-in packages, providing features such as advanced frame painting and motion-tracking tools. Finished work is compressed into QuickTime or Flash video formats for use on the web, or exported to broadcast-quality digital video.

Basic 3D animation tools can add motion to artwork such as logos for use on websites. For more advanced work, animation is supported alongside modeling and rendering by the major

3D applications, including NewTek's LightWave and Autodesk's Maya. Here the construction and motion of virtual lights and cameras become as significant as that of objects and backgrounds. To produce a complete spot, specialized plug ins may be required to generate certain elements and effects, and the final result will usually be further enhanced in postproduction software. When it comes to 3D animation, patience is a virtue: it's a long, exacting process. Serious bitmap and 3D animation place heavy demands on computers. Memory and hard disk requirements are large, and only the fastest processors and graphics cards will let you work with motion effects in real time. Nonetheless, an investment of less than $5,000 (£3,200) can equip a professional animation studio, and almost any personal computer can be used for Flash.

Right: "Onion-skinning" is a technique that's been transferred from traditional cel-based animation to digital. The software shows ghosts of the frames before and/or after the one you're currently editing, so you can make gradual adjustments to build up a smoothly animated sequence.
PICTURE: TOON BOOM STUDIO

Above: Animators will often mix tools and media to create the overall effect they're looking for. This music video for the Robbie Williams track "Let Love Be Your Energy" was created mostly in LightWave, but rendered to simulate 2D painted animation. The final look and editing of an animated spot may owe as much to video postproduction software as to the package used to generate the original animated content.
PICTURE: PASSION PICTURES/EMI

# DIGITAL PAINTING

PAINTING TECHNIQUES

HOW DIGITAL PAINTING WORKS

# 2

**THE PREMIER APPLICATION** for bitmap (paint) illustration is Adobe Photoshop. Although, as the name implies, the program is designed for retouching and montaging photographic images, Photoshop can be used to generate illustration work from scratch.

# HOW DIGITAL PAINTING WORKS

Adobe Photoshop's painting tools have a natural feel, particularly when used with a pressure-sensitive graphics tablet, and can be used for anything from freehand sketching to fully completed illustrations.

There are other photo-editing programs available, including Corel Photo-Paint and Corel Paintshop Pro, but Photoshop is the choice of the professional, offering a superb combination of power, reliability, and ease of use. This chapter will deal mainly with Photoshop, detailing its key strengths and capabilities.

Many illustrators use Photoshop for retouching and finishing off work begun in vector applications, adding texture and shading that would be too complex to create in a naturalistic manner in a vector environment. Artists working with 3D modeling applications frequently take their rendered output into Photoshop to correct modeling glitches, add backgrounds, and perform general compositing work. Although it would be possible—in theory, at least—to correct these factors directly in the 3D modeling environment, Photoshop avoids the sometimes lengthy rendering times by providing direct access to the image.

More recent versions of Photoshop have brought a new array of natural media brushes into play, which can be used to create work that looks as if it has been painted using traditional materials. Those artists wishing to specialize in this area may choose to work in Corel Painter instead (see page 42), which is dedicated to simulating a wide range of paint and drawing materials.

Opposite: This illustration for a feature on overweight America was created in Photoshop, using a photograph of the Statue of Liberty as its starting point. Although few readers would be fooled into thinking this was a real photograph, it has a degree of realism that wouldn't be possible using illustration alone.

**MANY OF THE FEATURES** of bitmap applications, such as Photoshop, are designed for re-touching photographs. They mimic the processes that would traditionally be carried out in a darkroom or during the reproduction process, as well as those made possible only by digital manipulation.

# Photographic manipulation

**2**

An understanding of photo manipulation techniques will help you prepare images obtained from scanned originals, digital photos, image libraries, and other sources. As well as maximizing the quality of your raw materials, you can also apply the same principles more creatively during the production of your artwork, whether for producing special effects, matching disparate images for montage, or simply ensuring that the final illustration is bright and crisp.

Endless mathematical operations can be carried out on the color values of pixels within your image. The most obviously useful are those corresponding to easily understood properties such as brightness, contrast, or hue. These are presented by the software in the form of sliders, with their effects on the image immediately visible as you drag the slider to increase or decrease the value.

For more clever and effective adjustments, the pixel values across the image can first be

This image (below left) may look satisfactory on-screen. However, when printed, the edges of the screw thread are softened and the metal texture is lost. Sharpening (center) recovers these details and gives a crisp appearance. Over-sharpening (right) produces speckling and fringes of false color; check carefully for these after each sharpening operation.

Above: This image looks washed-out, and a glance at its histogram in Photoshop confirms that its tonal range is limited—no pixels reach the darkest (left) or lightest (right) possible values.

Above: After applying Auto, the histogram is stretched, giving a much bolder result. Because Auto Levels can sometimes affect color balance, Auto Contrast and Auto Color are offered as alternatives.

plotted on a histogram (column chart). The axes can then be stretched or compressed to increase or limit the image's tonal range, or the midpoint shifted to change the balance of light and dark tones. This is performed using Photoshop's Levels control, which is typically used to correct images that look washed-out or "muddy," and offers an Auto option that can often provide instant improvements. Alternatively, the Curves control presents a graph on which average pixel values are represented by a diagonal line. You can then add points to this and move them, or redraw the line in any shape you choose, for subtle or dramatic tonal changes.

# Photographic manipulation

Filters offer even more complex adjustments. The most commonly used is Sharpening, where the software detects transitions between areas of different tone and adjusts pixels to emphasise the difference. The effect is to clarify detail. Since the printing process has a blurring effect, artwork destined for print will usually benefit from extra sharpening. A function known as Unsharp Mask helps achieve optimum results on a particular image.

Blurring is also supported, again supplemented by a more controllable alternative, Gaussian Blur. Bear in mind, though, that Blurring and Sharpening are not strictly opposites, and Sharpening will not rescue a badly blurred image, or Blurring an over-sharpened one. Other filters, often supplied as plug ins available either from the application's own manufacturer or from third parties, can be used to stylize images, simulate lighting effects, or create patterns, such as

The Curves dialog can reveal surprising hidden depths in the most innocuous of images. Here, several points have been manipulated to create multiple peaks and troughs, turning a bland blue sky into both a fantastic and sinister backdrop. Unnoticed graininess in the original photo has also become evident. However, this could be removed using a Blur or other filters.

Below: The Hue/Saturation/Lightness dialog box is a versatile tool, enabling global changes to be made directly to pixel values. Hue is what we would normally call the color spectrum. The scale is marked from 0° to 360°,

and you should imagine it being bent around in a circle, so that the left-hand side touches the right. This point represents cyan, and (from left to right) values pass through blue and purple to red in the middle, then through yellow and green on the way back to cyan. Saturation represents strength of color, from pale to bold. Lightness is self-explanatory. We will demonstrate the effects of different adjustments on this brightly colored image.

clouds, from scratch. Filters that create a specific appearance, like a bas-relief or oil painting, are often avoided by professional illustrators because they can detract from the originality of their work.

Exciting and innovative results can be generated by using filters in unexpected ways—for example, by applying extreme settings to distort an effect. Adjustments and filters are applied either to a whole image or to a selected area. An essential retouch tool that works rather differently is Cloning. You first click on a point within an image to pick up the surrounding pixels, and then paint elsewhere to apply them—the source point follows your brush, so an unlimited area can be duplicated. Cloning enables you to remove elements, such as deleting an irrelevant figure from a group photo, or duplicate them, turning a few figures into an army.

Below: Dragging the Master Hue slider to +120 (one-third of the way around the color wheel) shifts all colors from their original color wheel positions. The black-and-white pencils show no change.

Below: Selecting Green instead of Master applies the adjustment only to certain hues (defined by the color sliders). Now only the green "2" changes color. This technique can be used for subtle re-coloring.

Below: Shifting the Master Saturation to –50 washes out color across the board, leaving a range of grayish tones. Conversely, higher saturation will make for brighter, bolder images, though colors may start to look artificial.

**PHOTOMONTAGES** can be indistinguishable from real photographs. Alternatively, they can achieve a more artistic effect, with a result that could only be an illustration. Photomontage is the process of assembling illustrations using a variety of different images.

# Photomontage

Images may be scanned from photographic prints, captured using a digital camera, created using a 3D modeling application, or even drawn directly on the screen. In fact, photomontages do not necessarily have to include any photographs at all—it is the principle that counts. Each element in a photomontage is a separate layer, which can be manipulated independently of the others. Working this way means that it is possible to adjust the makeup of the montage as you go along. Elements can be moved, resized, re-colored, or removed entirely. It is only once you have completed the montage that you will need to "flatten" the layers into a single, composite image.

Unsurprisingly, Adobe Photoshop is the tool of choice for photomontage. Its selection, compositing, and layer-handling functions are powerful and highly sophisticated, enabling the

Left: This house was created by distorting a photograph of a brick wall to make the front and side walls; the same brick was darkened and distorted again to make the roof, and cropped to form the chimney stacks.

Below: Photographs of a door and window were distorted to match the perspective of the walls. The black inserts behind the window were created on a separate layer (see pages 48–53).

Left: A single drape was drawn in Photoshop, then textured, duplicated, and distorted to fit each window.

Right: The two "For Sale" signs were created as separate elements, and then distorted slightly using the Spherize filter once again.

user to manipulate images in just about any way imaginable. As the interface is quite intuitive, Photoshop is also relatively easy for the novice user to learn. Photoshop's own entry-level sibling, Photoshop Elements, has many of the same features at a much cheaper price, while rival applications such as Corel PaintShop Photo Pro can also produce excellent results.

When making montages, you will rarely use whole images in the composition—for example, you will often need to cut the desired component from its background. Selecting a particular portion of an image is done using a variety of tools—from simple rectangular and elliptical selections to tracings, using the Lasso tool, through to paths drawn with a Pen tool.

Below: This is the finished house, with all the elements in their correct positions.

To make the house look as though it fitted inside the crystal ball, it was distorted using Photoshop's Spherize filter.

# Photomontage

Photoshop also enables you to make selected areas of an image disappear, either by selecting all areas of a similar color and deleting them or by using special controls to hide all the areas that are darker or lighter than the value you specify. But be aware that deleting areas from a layer is an irrevocable step: once they are erased, you cannot retrieve them later. An alternative approach is to use a technique known as masking, in which portions of a layer are hidden rather than deleted. See pages 52–53 for more on this useful technique.

Done well a montage can look so realistic that it is difficult to discern from a single "real" photograph, or it can be more artistic, producing a finished result that is clearly an illustration. The example shown on these pages falls into the second category. Although most of the elements in it come from photographic sources, nobody would ever confuse it with a photograph.

Above: The ball itself was formed from a circular section taken from a photograph of a vase; the base is taken from a photograph of an Oscar trophy. The table beneath is simply a circular selection taken from a scan of a piece of wood.

Right: To add life to the crystal ball, this scan of a cloud was Spherized and then its layer mode changed (see page 50) so that only the brighter areas were visible.

Below: The head and hands were modeled in Poser (see page 138). The slightly unreal quality of

Poser models lent itself well to this kind of illustration.

Left: This image of a star field was placed in front of the head and hands layers, and its mode set so that only the dark background disappeared entirely.

Below: The finished illustration for Britain's Daily Telegraph newspaper was commissioned to accompany an article about realtors' difficulty in predicting the future of the housing market. The concept evolved through discussions with the section editor.

**COMPUTER APPLICATIONS** that can mimic the effects of natural media, such as watercolor and oil, are now coming into their own. They have the added bonus that anything you don't like can be erased from your canvas completely, enabling you to start again.

# Natural media

Although bitmap editors are sometimes referred to as paint programs, and provide tools with names like Brush and Pencil, only some tool behavior bears any notable resemblance to their real-world namesakes.

Accurate simulations of natural media such as inks and paints have proved difficult to program and are extremely demanding of computing power, leaving them low on the list of priorities when it comes to the development of mainstream software. For some users, however, particularly those converting traditional disciplines such as watercolor and pen and ink to digital illustration, these facilities are of paramount interest.

The leader in natural media for more than a decade has been Painter, a specialized application currently owned by Corel. Painter includes some adjustments and filters reminiscent of Photoshop, and can also make use of Photoshop plug-ins, but the majority of its features are dedicated to wet and dry brushes, pens, pencils, chalks, crayons, and other tools of the traditional artist. Particularly significant is the provision of wet watercolor layers, on which successive strokes can be left to run and bleed together as you paint. Not only is it possible to create highly realistic effects, but you can also carry out operations that would be impossible with real

media, such as erasing watercolor brush strokes and starting again.

To get the best from Painter, it is almost essential to invest in a graphics tablet. By linking stylus functions, such as pressure and tilt, to parameters such as the width and texture of brushstrokes, you can greatly increase the sense of physical interaction with the artwork. Drawing with the mouse is possible, but makes gestures unwieldy and relinquishes most of your real-time control over strokes. Many professional illustrators, who originally trained in media such as oils and airbrush, have successfully transferred their skills to Painter. The program is also widely used in the 2D departments of animation and movie studios, where it brings conventional visualization and rendering skills into the digital domain. Nonetheless, many users react to it with frustration. On screen, hundreds of controls are presented in a daunting and rather cumbersome list format.

When you start painting, different layers are created within your image depending on the kind of brush used, and each layer will then only respond to the application of appropriate brushes. The higher the resolution of your image, and the larger the brush you attempt to use, the slower the program will run. In practice, even modestly sized images will challenge the software to keep

The complex layering of color washes and fine brushstrokes in the leaf could only have been produced in Painter. At least two sets of veining detail have been drawn, one in fine, dark brushstrokes and another in erased color, suggesting superimposed images.

Created in Painter, this illustration demonstrates a number of techniques. Immediately obvious is the fact that it has been extensively worked and reworked. This is possible because the software lets successive strokes shift and distort what has already been painted.

Shading has been sketched onto the stalk using a very fine camel brush, effectively acting as a pen. The graphics tablet is ideal for fine detail such as this, and Painter's subtle blending and bleeding ensure the strokes are sufficiently integrated with the watercolor.

The edges here have been "burned" using a white eraser brush with a dark secondary color to catch the ocher paint, adding definition to this relatively light area. Further in, the ocher and green colors have been blended using a bleach brush.

A dry brush has been used to roughly scrape back the paint, adding textural interest. The increased contrast and definition make this area seem closer to the viewer's eye, and reinforce the perception that the object has three-dimensional depth.

A runny wash has been applied to this area using a dark color. The primary purpose of this is to add shadow, but it also blurs the underlying strokes, helping to give an impression of selective focus on the brighter part of the apple.

# Natural media

up with you. However, as Painter is developed further and computing power continues to climb, many of these issues are likely to be resolved in the future.

No other application goes as far in this context, but some general-purpose bitmap editors do offer brushes that can be used and edited creatively. In Photoshop, for example, brushes can each incorporate two different elements overlaid using any of the usual blending modes, with size, spacing, opacity, and color independently set to change randomly or in response to stylus functions. You will not get your strokes to blend and bleed together as you will with Painter, but impressive results can nevertheless still be obtained, particularly if creative experimentation is more important to you than mimicking specific real-world techniques.

Left: Painter's user interface is a little disorienting at first, with an unfamiliar structure and all too many options lurking within the list-based toolboxes. Once you start painting, however, you will gradually get a feel for the options you need and where to look for them.

DIGITAL PAINTING

Right: Photoshop's brush technology has its strengths. This layered brush (top) gives an abstract effect that would be harder to achieve in Painter, and its extensive settings can all be found in one place for easy editing. But Painter excels when it comes to mimicking real media. Here (bottom) a notched palette knife is being used to smear thick impasto onto the paper, producing almost three-dimensional artwork.

Right: Painter's Watercolor brushes closely simulate the running together of multiple strokes of wet paint (top). Note the distinct bristle pattern and the way this is blurred by the addition of yellow paint on top. An equivalent brush in Photoshop (bottom) produces a vaguely brushlike effect, but with far less definition and no attempt to blend successive strokes. On the other hand, the Photoshop example was much quicker to create.

**PIXEL ART** is a form of illustration that turns the conventional approach to bitmap editing on its head. Rather than using high resolutions and careful manipulation to prevent the "bitmapped" nature of the artwork becoming evident, pixel artists celebrate the digital medium by working at very low resolutions, using pixels as building blocks to construct often detailed, but always conspicuously bitmapped, images.

# Pixel art

**2**

Since modern bitmap applications were not developed with this purpose in mind, they offer few relevant features. Selection and Fill tools can be used, provided that their anti-aliasing option is turned off, as it has the effect of disguising pixels rather than leaving them intact. Line drawing tools can be used for 90° and 45° lines, but their results are too unpredictable at other angles. Accordingly, the initial drawing process is generally little more sophisticated than placing individual pixels of different colors one at a time. Since this is extremely labor intensive, artists will duplicate elements (whether within the current artwork or from previ-

ous jobs) as often as they draw new ones. While working, elements can be set aside on separate layers or as alpha channels, ready for reuse.

Any subject can be tackled, but a popular sub-genre is isometrics, a form of perspective traditionally used in technical drawing. Based on 30° angles, this method simplifies the construction of 3D objects in 2D artwork, and its abstract, diagrammatic nature helps create a characteristic feel. Shading is added to heighten the semi-realistic effect, and the one-pixel black outlines with which elements are drawn are usually retained as part of the final artwork.

Left: Unfortunately, standard bitmap drawing tools are of little help in constructing pixel art. Photoshop's Line tool is anti-aliased by default (left), and even when anti-aliasing is turned off, the results (middle) are unsatisfactory because pixels are not evenly distributed. Only a painstaking process of placing individual pixels with the Pencil tool will generate the perfectly clean effect required (right).

Right: Pixel art is typically based on a modified form of isometric drawing. A true isometric grid has lines at 30° angles on either side of the vertical. When these lines are bitmapped, the aliasing effect breaks them into an irregular sequence of one- and two-pixel segments. For a neater appearance, pixel artists draw lines at 22.5° angles. Just as a 45° line is formed from evenly stepped single pixels, a line at half this angle proceeds in two-pixel steps. The result is not a true isometric drawing, but looks similar.

DIGITAL PAINTING

A restricted color palette is often used. This may be defined by the artist, or an existing palette may be applied, one choice being the so-called web-safe palette. This is a set of 216 colors that are supposed to display correctly on almost any web-capable computer. However, as an increasing number of computers support millions of colors, and web design trends demand the use of high-color photographic images that cannot be made web safe, the system is already close to obsolete. Despite that, it does still provide an esthetically interesting selection of shades.

When editing, re-purposing, or reproducing pixel art, take care not to compromise its bit-mapped format. Re-sampling will normally involve interpolation, which breaks down the pixel structure. For this reason, the resolution of such illustrations must never be reduced. If resolution needs to be increased—for example, to increase the size of the pixels when displayed on a web site—this should always be done in whole multiples of 100% and with re-sampling disabled (in Photoshop, this can be done by selecting Nearest Neighbor, rather than Bicubic or Bilinear Interpolation).

A number of related genres exploit digital characteristics through various means. In ASCII art, for example, photos or even video clips are converted into grids of letters and numbers, using the relative "darkness" of different characters (a dash would be very light, an M very dark) in place of pixel values. Although this is an automated process, serious practitioners write their own software routines for the conversion, and in the process introduce an element of creativity. Other illustrators set arbitrary limits on their work, such as using only basic geometric shapes or working to a fixed grid, whether in bitmap or vector form.

Left: In this part of the illustration (above), the artists play with pixel art conventions by enabling parts of the building to explode out of their isometric constraints. Even within the flames, however, a restricted color palette is used, and edges are not anti-aliased.

Left: FlipFlopFlyin's Minipops are an extreme example of bitmap art, using just a few pixels to construct miniscule portraits of ZZ Top.

**WHILE THE BASICS** of paint applications such as Adobe Photoshop are fairly simple to grasp, it is once you delve into their more complex aspects that you truly unlock their potential for illustrations.

# PAINTING TECHNIQUES

Getting to grips with Photoshop's layers, masks, and effects filters will pay dividends in the end. By learning to work with layers you immediately open up a range of compositional possibilities. Add Layer Effects and the Lighting Effects filters to your repertoire and you can lend your work a new, three-dimensional edge. You can even combine your paper artwork with Photoshop to add color and shade the easy way, with the power and flexibility of digital techniques and the safety net of a single-click Undo. And should you reach the limits of your chosen application's capabilities, there is a host of third-party plug ins waiting to expand your options even further.

A new document starts with just one layer, referred to as the Background, which is filled with white. When you add a layer, its pixels are transparent, so anything on the background shows through. Anything you add to the layer, whether by painting or pasting elements from other files, appears on top of the background. As you add more layers, each appears on top of the last. Each layer is listed on-screen in a palette, and any one of them can be visible or invisible. This means that you can work on a single layer at a time or check what the artwork would look like without it. One layer is the "active" layer at any time, and any operations you carry out apply only to it. This means that, when you make a selection, only pixels in the active layer are selected—moving or otherwise transforming the selection will not affect the layers on top or underneath. Copying and pasting the selection normally creates a new layer containing only the selected material. This can then be positioned independently.

Right: Representation of Photoshop's Layers.

**WORKING WITH LAYERS** In applications such as Adobe Photoshop, layers are central to the working methods of most illustrators. By maintaining elements of artwork as separate entities, while controlling how they combine to form the whole composite result, layers bring practical and creative advantages to digital painting.

# Layers

Layers can be grouped into sets, which can then be repositioned together. Later, layers can be permanently merged with others, and ultimately the whole document can be flattened into a single composite image ready for reproduction. But although layers appear on top of each other, this is not a complete description of the way they combine. Each layer has an Opacity and a Blending mode, which together determine exactly how its pixels interact with those of underlying layers.

In Normal mode, pixels in a higher layer simply overwrite those underneath, to the degree dictated by the higher layer's opacity. However, in other modes, a mathematical formula is applied to determine color values. Darken, for example, replaces only pixels that were lighter than the ones being overlaid, leaving darker pixels intact.

Multiply, meanwhile, creates a more subtle effect by multiplying the color values of the new and underlying pixels, giving a darkening effect. Screen does the opposite, multiplying the inverse of the color values for a lighter result, while Hard Light multiplies where the new pixels are dark and screens where they are light, creat-

When the Clouds layer is set to Hard Light mode (left), it lets the underlying artwork show through (right) and adds an overall texture to the illustration, unifying the disparate elements. The Clouds layer (left) obscures the entire artwork when placed at the top of the composition (right). The Spaceship layer (left) simply sits on top of the Earth layer in the composition (right). The Earth layer is positioned off the "canvas" (left), but can still be retrieved if desired—in this composition (right), it is cropped by the canvas size. The Stars layer sits at the very bottom of the stack to form the background.

DIGITAL PAINTING

ing an exaggerating effect similar to a spotlight. There are many more modes to choose from.

A further refinement of layers in Photoshop is incorporating adjustment layers. Most adjustments (such as Brightness and Contrast) that you might apply to an image can instead be applied to an adjustment layer. This layer does not contain any pixels, but instead carries information about the adjustment, which then affects pixels in all the layers below it. You can therefore apply effects without committing to them permanently—the

Above: When the sky image (above far left) is layered over the wire fence (second left), you can see the result obtained with the following blending modes: Darken, Lighten, Overlay, and Vivid Light.

adjustment layer's settings can be edited later—while the actual pixels in other layers remain intact throughout, with only the appearance of the composite artwork changing. This is great because it lets you experiment radically with illustrations in a completely reversible way.

**LAYER MASKS** let you hide and reveal different aspects of an image. But the best thing is that the technique is totally reversible. The easiest way to remove part of an unwanted layer in your image is to delete it. This is fine when you are sure you want to lose elements permanently, for example, when cutting an object from its background and being certain that you will not want to retrieve the background at a later point.

# Layer masks

Deleting (making a selection and pressing the Delete key) and erasing (using the Eraser tool to paint out areas) are irrevocable steps, and should be used with caution. A better solution is to create a mask for the layer, which hides parts of that layer without deleting them. The advantage is that you can selectively hide areas and, if necessary, bring them back later. This is the best way of keeping your options open, since you do not need to commit to a permanent deletion.

A layer mask is a grayscale image that affects the visibility of the layer to which it is attached. Any black areas on the mask will hide those parts of the layer, while white areas will enable the layer's other selections to remain visible. Gray areas render the layer semi-visible—the darker the gray, the more hidden those areas will be.

The easiest way to make a mask is to paint with the Brush—it is as easy as using the Eraser. Painting with a hard-edged brush will create a sharp cut-off between the visible and the hidden, whereas painting with a soft brush will make that part of the layer gradually fade away. Unlike using the Lasso tool, you do not need to trace a complete outline in one go, as masks can be painted in small sections to increasingly hide the layer with each brushstroke. Switching the foreground (painting) color from black to white will enable you to paint the layer back in again in exactly the

same way. This makes it easy to perform complex cut-outs, since you do not need to worry about deleting areas that you want to retain—it is a simple matter to paint them back in again.

Masks can be created with any of the painting tools—not just the Brush. Use the Gradient tool to make a gradual fade in any direction, or the Smudge tool to tweak out strands of grass, hair, leaves, and so on. You can also make selections within the mask using the Lasso or Marquee tools, and fill them with black to hide large areas without having to laboriously paint them out.

Normally, the layer mask will be linked to the layer, and will move with it. But as the pipe and ring example on the opposite page shows, it is possible to separate the two so that they operate independently. In this way, it is possible to make the pipe appear to be both in front of and behind the ring layer simultaneously, as it appears to pass through it.

A counterpart to layer masks is QuickMask, a selection mode that works in exactly the same way. You enter QuickMask mode by pressing Q. You can then use any of the painting tools, just as if you were painting a mask. In this mode, the solid mask will be shown as a translucent red rather than black (so you can see what you are doing). When you exit QuickMask by pressing Q again, the painted area will become a selection.

Left: This pipe is in front of the ring layer; the layer mask has been made on just the left side of the ring, obscuring that section of the pipe.

   pipe

Center left: When the pipe is moved, the mask moves with it. This is because the layer is linked to its mask (above), which can be seen in the tiny chain symbol between the two in the top layer on the Layers palette.

Left: When the link is broken, the two components operate independently. Now, we can move the pipe wherever we like, and the mask will stay where it is.

Above and above right: This box was positioned on a beach background. It did not look like it belonged there at all, so a layer mask was made and part of the box painted out. The foreground color was switched from black to white to paint the box back in again. By using a low opacity for the brush, the hidden area was partially revealed so that the box is seen through the water. A brush mode called "dissolve" paints rough, dotty edges. It was put to good use here, to paint the box mask around the sand in a more convincing manner.

Below: Here is the finished mask seen alone, showing the dotted edges around the sand. The gray area on the right creates the semi-transparent edge of the box.

**THE TERM** "Photomontage" can cover a range of artistic styles, from the truly photographic to the entirely illustrative. In this example, we look at an image that falls halfway between the two: while photographic in treatment, it is clearly not a real photograph.

# Photomontage

This image was commissioned for the cover of the "Review" section of Britain's Independent newspaper. When combining images from a variety of sources, the key to creating a successful montage lies in making all the elements blend together convincingly. The elements do not need to come from the same, or even a similar, source. Here, the fork was photographed with a digital camera, the map outline was a PostScript map with all the detail removed, and the steak came from a royalty-free photography collection.

If you are working on complex montages that contain many elements, it is possible to end up with dozens of separate layers. So, to avoid confusion, it is worth naming the layers as you create them—in this case, they might be called "steak," "fat mask," "fork prongs," and so on. It takes just a few seconds to name each layer, and it can avoid a mass of confusion later on.

Photoshop also enables layers to be grouped together in sets, without affecting their appearance, making navigation that much easier. In addition, entire sets can be turned on and off with a single click, making it possible to build multiple variations of a montage in a single file and flip between them instantly.

1. To begin this image, a silhouette of a map of England, Scotland, and Wales is rotated to fit on top of a cutout photograph of a fork. This will form the basis for the steak shape.

2. This photograph of a piece of steak is positioned on top of the map. It doesn't quite cover it, but it's easy enough to clone areas to where they're wanted.

3. When the steak is "grouped" with the map layer, it shows up only where it overlaps the map. The steak now takes on the shape of the map perfectly.

DIGITAL PAINTING

4. The map layer is duplicated, and offset to provide some thickness to the steak. This layer is then sent to the back, behind the original map.

5. Now a piece of the fat from the edge of the original steak is copied to a new layer, and grouped with the "thickness" layer. Elements of the fat are moved around so that they fill the layer completely.

6. A further layer of the fat is copied and grouped with a new mask, painted roughly around the edge of the whole map, so that the fat now runs all the way around the steak.

7. A new adjustment layer enables us to darken the steak. By painting irregular diagonal lines on the mask for this layer, we can give the impression of the steak being newly grilled.

8. A copy of the end of the fork is made on a new layer, and brought to the front. This is then masked so that the fork appears to be pressing through the steak. Shadows, both on the steak and on the fork, add to the realism.

**AUTOSHADING AND 3D** shading can provide flat images with depth and dimension, and add contours and texture to objects. The process requires some trial and error, but the end results are always rewarding. Artists traditionally create the impression of 3D by painting highlights and shadows.

# Beveling and embossing

Software packages provide various features to automate the process, which can be used very effectively to simulate two-and-a-half-dimensional or bas-relief materials and objects. The most basic form of autoshading is beveling or embossing. This works by "offsetting" existing information in an image. Superimposing a lightened copy shifted up and left, or a darkened copy shifted in the opposite direction (down and right), gives the impression of light falling across an object from the top left corner. Scaling shaded copies of an image outward gives the effect of a flattened pyramid, reminiscent of a button—for

example, a key on a computer keyboard. More complex profiles can be built up by varying the offsets, while a more softened result can be achieved by applying a "blur" to the image.

Bitmap programs and plug ins combine these processes into filters that are dedicated to producing certain types of bevel or contour. In Photoshop, for example, the most flexible beveling tools are found in the Layer Effects module, in which contours can be edited to govern the exact shape being represented.

Although beveling has been over-used in contexts such as website navigation buttons, it

Left: Various techniques can be used to generate simple highlights and shadows. The simplest is to intersect offset copies of an object in opposite directions, then darken and lighten them. This process is automated by Photoshop's Emboss filter, with primitive results (left to center), then manipulated with Gaussian Blur for effect (right).

Left: Shading can be processed in various ways to change its appearance. Trial and error with Photoshop's Curves can give effects like shiny (left) and glassy (center). If photorealism is not required, tonal range can be reduced using Posterize (right) for pop-art effects. Plug ins are available to create a range of predefined and customized results.

DIGITAL PAINTING

Altering the pattern of light, dark, and blurring in the texture channel changes the profile of the virtual object rendered by Lighting Effects. An existing alpha channel can be adjusted using the Curves control. Here, different alpha channels created from a basic blurred disc create a simple rounded edge (left), a rounded edge with additional outer shading that avoids highlighted edges disappearing into the background (middle), and a simulated paint can lid (right).

remains a versatile technique with many useful applications. For example, soft bevels can add a subtle sense of depth to flat shapes within a composition, an effect now routinely seen in cartoons—where it is applied using specialized plugins—and mimicked in cartoon-like illustration and character-development work.

More advanced pseudo-3D shading can be achieved with tools such as Photoshop's Lighting Effects, which casts a glow over an image from one or more chosen directions. In itself, this is a 2D effect, but it can be applied through an "alpha" channel to create a complex contour. An alpha channel is a separate grayscale image, similar to a layer mask. Image pixels are shifted according to the value of each corresponding pixel in the alpha channel, with darker areas appearing higher in the contour. Pixel values are further adjusted according to the color and strength of the light at each point. Although this isn't a true 3D operation, it can be used to transform a few simple shapes into a highly realistic semi-3D object.

The Lighting Effects filter offers a large number of sliders, which need to be used carefully to

# Beveling and embossing

produce the desired result. The position, intensity, and focus of the light must be balanced against the overall exposure and ambience to avoid the image being plunged into gloom or being "whited out." Two sliders control the surface properties of the object being rendered, varying from matte to shiny and from plastic (soft) to metallic (hard). These will also affect overall tonal range, and extreme values may create unwanted artifacts—patterns generated by the software—in the finished result.

More important still is the pre-processing of your alpha channel. Although you will usually create your object as a simple black-on-white shape, you will need to apply some Blur: this provides a transition from high to low in the contour, which would otherwise jump unrealisti-

cally from maximum to minimum. Further adjustment using Levels or Curves will dictate the exact shape of the contour.

Texture can also be added at this stage with a "texture" channel. The Noise filter randomizes the values of a certain proportion of pixels within an image, giving a speckled or grainy effect. A small amount of noise added to your alpha channel will produce a stippled surface when Lighting Effects is applied. More noise gives a rougher surface, while blurring the noise gives a beaten effect.

Some trial and error will be required to achieve good results with Lighting Effects, but the effort is usually rewarded. Having successfully completed a task, it is well worth saving the lighting setup and noting the amount of Blur, Noise, and other adjustments used.

Left: The text and outline are created in an alpha channel (see previous spread). The channel itself is loaded as a selection, and the smaller text is subtracted from this. The Noise filter is used to lightly speckle the text and outline, but not the background. A small Gaussian Blur is then applied to soften the noise to a mottled effect (inset). The smaller text is then treated with lesser amounts of noise and blur.

DIGITAL PAINTING

**Lighting Effects**

Style: 2 o'clock Spotlight

Save... | Delete | OK | Cancel

Light Type: Spotlight

☑ On

Intensity: Negative | 10 | Full

Focus: Narrow | 100 | Wide

**Properties**

Gloss: Matte | 10 | Shiny

Material: Plastic | 100 | Metallic

Exposure: Under | –18 | Over

Ambience: Negative | 16 | Positive

Texture Channel: Bump map

☑ White is high

Height: Flat | 28 | Mountainous

Preview

Above: The alpha channel is then chosen as the texture channel for the Lighting Effects filter. This creates the illusion of a 3D object by offsetting light and dark pixels. The greater the contrast, the deeper the texture. Various sliders control the apparent depth of the object, as well as the color, direction, strength, and breadth of the light striking it. Several different lights can be used for more complex compositions.

Right: This generates the basic shading, with the smaller text appearing smoother and flatter than the street name and outline. Further work is needed to progress from an even, mid-gray image to the full-color sign. The alpha channel is used to separate the text and border from the background; the street name is darkened and the background lightened using Levels, then the smaller text is colored using Hue/Saturation.

HOWEVER MUCH you may be used to your mouse or graphics tablet, there are times when only a pencil and real, old-fashioned paper are up to the job. Artists coming from a traditional illustration background will find drawing on paper more natural than trying to get smooth lines from a mouse. In cases like these, you'll need to scan your artwork and color it afterward.

# Coloring artwork

Scanned line artwork will often appear with rather low contrast, with the lines a darkish gray against a pale gray background. This is particularly true of pencil sketches. Rather than attempting to get a better scan, it's easy to fix this in Adobe Photoshop: use the Brightness and Contrast controls, increasing them both until you end up with crisp black lines against a clean, white background.

There are two ways of selecting areas to be filled with color: Paint Bucket and the Magic Wand. Paint Bucket will "pour" color into any bordered area, and is the simplest method. However, because of the imperfect transition between the pure black of the outlines and the pure white of the interior, you'll usually find a faint white fringe

remains inside all the black outlines. In addition, filling in this way will mean coloring directly onto the scanned outline layer. It's far better to keep the outline and color component as separate layers, to give you maximum flexibility later.

For these reasons, it's generally better to use the Magic Wand tool, which selects areas but doesn't fill them. Then simply expand the selection by a pixel or two (to make sure your color extends right into the outlines) and, switching to your "color" layer, fill with the color of your choice. Switch back to the "outline" layer to make further selections, and continue this process.

One problem with both the Paint Bucket and Magic Wand solutions is "leakage." Both tools will color or select areas that are wholly bounded

Far left: Scanning line artwork, such as this simple pencil sketch, will often result in a washed-out image with a dirty gray background.

Left: Increasing the brightness and contrast in Photoshop will help to salvage the image. You may need to paint out stray black dots as well.

DIGITAL PAINTING

Above: Here's our baseline artwork typical of the sort of image that would be drawn on paper before being scanned in. Because we're going to auto-select the areas, we need to plug any holes in the outlines. Gaps would make selections hard to achieve.

Above right: Select areas to be filled with the Magic Wand tool, and enlarge the selection by a pixel or two. Then, on a new layer, fill with your chosen color.

Right: The rest of the artwork can be colored in the same way. It can help to make multiple layers for each color element, to make it easier to adjust them later.

by their outlines—that is, they select contiguous areas of the same color. But if your drawing style involves leaving gaps in these outlines, the selections will leak out through these gaps and fill or select the neighboring area as well—which may include the entire background.

The solution is to duplicate the outline layer once you've scanned it in, and use a small paintbrush to plug the gaps. This doesn't mean you need to change your drawing style: simply use this new layer for the purpose of making selections. After you've filled all the color areas,

you can discard this new layer and return to the original. You'll find now, however, that because the selection areas were enlarged by that pixel or two, your outlines will be thinner than they were before. This is easily remedied: duplicate the original outline layer once more, and move the new layer to the top of the stack. As it stands, it will obscure all the coloring. But if you change its layer mode from Normal to Multiply, the white component (the background paper) will disappear entirely, enabling you to see the color elements underneath.

**EMULATING THE STYLE** of great artists is often easier on a computer than it is by any other means. While knocking out a quick Rembrandt or Caravaggio may be out of the reach of most illustrators, pop art lends itself well to digital techniques. Here, we look at how to create images in the style of Andy Warhol and Roy Lichtenstein.

# DIY pop art

To make this image, it's important to start with the right kind of photograph. You need to use one that's well contrasted, with strong shadows; a bland, front-lit photograph will prove much harder to work with. The technique we'll use here involves taking several copies of the image and applying different degrees of "thresholding" to them—a way of converting a scanned photograph to pure black and white—to make the different layers of shading in the image.

1. This is the original head for our "Warholesque" image. There are many sources of suitable images; this one is taken from a royalty-free photograph collection.

2. Begin by duplicating this layer (we'll need to use it later), and fill with a suitable flesh color. You can fill a selection with the foreground color in Photoshop by pressing Option+Delete (Alt+Delete).

3. Now duplicate the original layer again, and set its mode to Multiply. This causes the new layer to darken those beneath it: bright areas will not be affected, as we'll see later.

DIGITAL PAINTING

4. Use the Threshold dialog to turn the new layer into pure black and white. By moving the slider, we can control the cutoff point; here we're creating the deep shadows, so we want to see only the darkest regions.

5. Duplicate the original layer again. Set its mode to Multiply and repeat the Threshold dialog, moving the slider so more of the image is seen. When we colorize this layer, we'll make a second shadow layer.

6. Paint the hair on a new layer. Set the mode of this layer to Color, and it will change the hue of the underlying layers without brightening them, so that the shading is still seen beneath.

7. The color for the pupils and the eyeshadow is applied in the same way. It's worth creating all these elements on separate layers, so that it's easier to edit them and change the colors later.

8. Using Color mode for the "lips" layer will produce a washed-out effect: we want the lips to be good and strong. Setting the layer mode to Multiply works much better in this particular instance.

9. While it would be possible to paint the white teeth and eyes on a new layer, it's easier to adjust them on the "base (fleshtone)" layer. Use the Dodge tool set to highlights to brighten up these areas. Finally, add a couple of dabs of red in the cheeks.

# DIY pop art

1. This is the starting point for our Lichtenstein-style image. It's a straight-forward image of a plane, taken from a royalty-free clip art collection.

2. On a new Photoshop layer, paint in the shading on the plane. Set the new layer's mode to Multiply and you'll be able to see through it to the plane's detail below.

3. Now duplicate that layer, and use the Color Halftone filter to add the dots. The default screen angles in the resulting dialog will match those of halftone printing; set them all to 45° for this graphic effect.

4. Fill the background with blue, then make a new gray-filled layer and repeat the previous filter. The clouds are simply painted in white on a new layer.

5. To make the flame, first draw a path with the Pen tool. Hit Enter to make it into a selection, and fill with a fire color.

6. Now draw another, slightly smaller path inside the original flame. When you hit Enter, only the border will be selected. Fill this with black.

DIGITAL PAINTING

7. Add more layers of flame in exactly the same way, following the previous two steps.

8. Add the caption text, and draw a bubble behind it following the technique used for drawing the flames.

Comic-book paintings are easy to create with a suitable starting image. The key lies in choosing the right font for the lettering. Here, we've used Tekton— now supplied with most computer operating systems—for the caption, and Comics Cartoon—available as part of shareware collections, or variations on it—for the large text.

9. The large lettering needs to be "rasterized" (converted to a standard layer) so that the letters can be rearranged to overlap each other.

IN THE LATE 1990S, a new genre of digital illustration emerged. Although associated with fast-rising agencies such as Attik, it seemed to spring from all quarters at once, including a generation of graphics students graduating from the new technology-oriented programs.

# Multilayer illustration

**2**

Rich in detail, depth, and texture, stacking image upon image, and eschewing direct references to its subject matter, this fresh abstract style—known to some as "line action" for its typical embellishment with repeated rules, grids, and circles—was a controversial but exciting development only made possible by using digital methods. In fact, what made it possible was the introduction of layers into Adobe Photoshop. Once users could keep elements separate from each other yet seamlessly combined, trial and error in compositing became immeasurably more productive and, potentially, creative. Along with rising computer power and new sources of raw material—including the Internet, royalty-free photo libraries, affordable scanners, and user-friendly 3D software—the arrival of layers rapidly triggered an explosion of experimentation.

Of course, not all experiments have desirable outcomes. When setting out to create this type of illustration, a good eye and sense of conceptual design are of even greater importance than with conventional artwork, since there are fewer barriers between the artist and a meaningless jumble. As with collage or photomontage, the starting point is usually not a blank canvas but a collection of raw material, probably centering on an image or form that has triggered the creative process in an illustrator who is searching for a concept.

The relationship between the artwork and the concept may be rather vague, however, and it is no coincidence that abstract digital pieces are often produced on spec and then sold to clients later, either as is or modified to fit a particular project. The illustration constructed on these pages, for example, is taken from a collection commissioned and marketed by a picture library—art directors buy the image as a Photoshop PSD file with layers intact, and can edit or subtract elements, or combine layers from different files, to customize the artwork to their specifications.

Lacking the overt metaphors and visual puns characteristic of mainstream illustration, such images have to find new ways of engaging the viewer's interest. Striking visual forms, whether explosive patterns of light or evocative geometric or organic constructions, are often used to grab attention. These provide the foreground, often arranged in deliberate opposition to traditional ideas of composition, with large areas left blank. Behind, dense layers of additional material expand to the edges of the canvas and recede seemingly into infinity.

Here, some old-fashioned artists' tricks come into play: the illusion of depth is created by dimming, lightening, de-saturating, or blurring elements, and the impression of movement by repeating objects at different scales, colors, and opacities. Frenzied "line action" can work in a way similar to the cartoonist's "whizz" lines, or in calmer examples may give a feeling of drifting motion, an effect more literally realized in related genres of animated web design.

A sound understanding of the various layer types and modes is essential, and best developed through experience. Blending modes, such as Burn, Light, and Overlay, are particularly useful for building up dense imagery, as they preserve the contributions of underlying layers. Hard-edged foreground elements can be cut out using transparency or layer masks. Adjustment layers can change the color or brightness of certain elements—bound into clipping groups to limit their effect—or of the entire artwork, while leaving the imagery itself intact and all options open for later changes.

But there are still some limits imposed by the technology on all this unfettered creativity. While file sizes of single images are determined by their resolution, the amount of data in a layered document is unlimited. Photoshop's intelligent memory management ensures you will not be prevented from working with an image, but even on systems with a fast processor and a gigabyte of RAM, a heavily layered A4-plus file can slow performance. It is often useful to save a full copy of your artwork in its current state, then merge together any layers you are unlikely to want to change, leaving a less cumbersome document on which to continue working.

Image from gform 1.26 by Bradley Grosh and Anders Schroeder, in the Infinity collection from Digital Vision.
WWW.DIGITALVISIONONLINE.CO.UK

# Multilayer illustration

Right: Here, several 3D elements have been combined to suggest both organic and technological forms. Objects such as these can be modeled in a 3D package and rendered out as bitmap files, or created within Photoshop using pseudo-3D tools such as beveling plug ins. A characteristic feature is that the shapes are wildly distorted, giving an impression of exaggerated perspective that draws the eye into the image.

Opposite top: The main 2D elements are simple colored shapes, which can be drawn in Photoshop or imported from a drawing package. Blending modes such as Color Burn and Luminosity are used where shapes are required to show through each other. Although the 2D work is seen here in bitmap layers, it is also possible to use vector layers, enabling free scaling without loss of quality. Vector shapes can be rendered to pixels in the event that bitmap filters need to be applied. This is how the initial composition looks. The 3D layers are higher up the stacking order. Normal mode is used to overwrite underlying pixels, but layer masks restrict each layer to the shape it contains, letting surrounding areas show through (layer masks are shown to the right of each layer's content in the Layers palette). The background layer is filled with a gradient traveling from light blue at the bottom to white at the top. This is modified by an adjustment layer (01) carrying a Levels function, which in turn is restricted by a layer mask containing a diagonal gradient. By graduating the adjustment at an angle to the fill, a subtler color wash is created.

Opposite middle: Layer 29 is an adjustment layer set to Invert. Adjustment layers affect all underlying layers, so it turns the whole artwork to different extents into a negative image, changing its feel from bright to threatening. One of the benefits of adjustment layers is that you can experiment with dramatic changes such as this without committing to them. For now, the immediate problem is that key elements have become pink instead of blue. This will be corrected using Hue/Saturation with Colorize in an extra adjustment layer (33). Applying the same hue across the whole artwork helps make visual sense of the frenzied composition.

Opposite bottom: Text is added (in this case, purely for decorative purposes) in a number of additional layers, using Normal mode with varying opacity. Type layers in Photoshop have the same choice of blending modes and opacity levels as ordinary layers, while text remains fully editable and re-sizeable. The artwork is completed by adding a half dozen extra layers containing subtle shading, blurred duplicates of some key elements, and a graph paper background; these are each added in layers arranged appropriately in the stacking order.

DIGITAL PAINTING

Left: The number and diversity of layers in the palette may make this image look dauntingly complex, but they make it much simpler to work with. Since each layer can be turned on and off at will, and its content edited independently, changes to one element or aspect of the artwork can be made without affecting others, and without having to repeat tricky masking operations.

# DIGITAL DRAWING

# 3

# DRAWING PRINCIPLES

**DRAWING** with a vector-based application requires a different approach to the bitmap-based packages we have discussed earlier.

Vector drawings are built from simple elements, combined into objects, that together form finished drawings. We build the simplest element—the path—from Bézier curves. By applying strokes and fills we give that path shape, color, and form, producing an object from the outline. Through arranging, stacking, and layering objects it is possible to produce a drawn image, but with one crucial difference. Each object can be edited, transformed, and resized independently, giving us plentiful scope to experiment and rework.

This way of drawing takes time and practice before it can be mastered. Working with Bézier curves might prove tricky to those more used to the traditional ways of pen and ink. The approach can feel far less intuitive, and even clinical. However, you will soon discover quick ways of producing complex shapes, while more advanced strokes and fills bring a number of great creative possibilities within your reach. Gradient fills, transparency effects and blend modes can make your illustrations even more eye-catching, and every shading effect you can produce on paper has its equivalent in the digital realm. The same cannot be said the other way round.

That is not all. As objects can also be copied and used again and again, the vector approach can also be a major time saver. Why draw every window in a building when you can simply copy, transform, and rescale just a few?

Opposite: Even the most basic vector drawing is based on a number of paths, themselves comprised of multiple Bézier curves. Producing such an object is a complex business, but once created this hand can be transformed or resized at will.

**BÉZIER CURVES** use complex mathematical models to help digital illustrators draw curves, corners, circles, and arches more easily. Practice is required, but they are not as daunting as they might first appear. All Vector drawing software is based on Bézier curves, which are each defined by four points: the start and end points, or nodes, and two control points, or handles.

# Bézier curves

Behind the scenes, various different mathematical models are used to construct the curves, but the general principle is that curves tend toward their handles while never passing through them. Continuous curves, or paths, are composed of multiple Bézier segments, each moving on from the last one's end point. Two control handles are arranged on a parallel line through this point, forming a tangent to the curve. This is referred to as a curve point, and the curve passes smoothly through it. If necessary, you can move one of the handles further away than the other, making an asymmetrical curve. Or you can adjust the handles independently, making the curve turn sharply, in which case the point becomes a corner point.

Using your software's pen tool, draw paths by clicking with the mouse wherever you want the next point. Clicking and letting go places a point with no handles; repeating this action forms a series of straight lines. To draw curves, you click to place a point, then drag away from it while still holding down the mouse button. This forms a curve by pulling out a handle, for the first point

**Bézier curves 1. Curves and corners**
In this example we'll draw a pair of arches, showing how to form simple curves and corners using the Bézier pen.

1. Having clicked once to make the first point, click where you want the second point, and keep the mouse button held down.

2. Drag the pointer to pull out a curve handle; the other handle follows it symmetrically on the opposite side of the point.

3. Let go, then click where you want the third point, forming a two-part curve, and let go immediately, to make a corner.

on the path, or two symmetrical handles, for all other points. If you click at the end of a curve without dragging, a point with no handles appears, and the next line or curve can continue at a sharp angle. So the basic rules are: click + click = straight line; drag + drag = smooth curve; drag + click = broken curve.

When you've finished your path, you can either click on the first point again to complete an enclosed shape, known as a closed path, or switch tools and click away from the path to leave it as an open line.

As the examples below demonstrate (seen here in Adobe Illustrator), this is all quite straightforward in practice. If Bézier curves seem a little mysterious at first, that's hardly surprising, they are quite mysterious mathematical beasts. There are no exact methods, for example, of drawing a circle using Bézier curves, or drawing concentric curves. But software developers have found sufficiently accurate approximations, and the way vector drawing tools work on screen is both compre-

hensible and efficient after a small amount of trial and error.

To provide a framework for accurate drawing, vector applications offer guides and grids. Grids are the digital version of graph paper, displayed either behind or in front of your artwork. You can set the grid units, such as every half inch (1 cm) or every 5 cm (2 inches), and the number of subdivisions within this. Guides are horizontal or vertical lines that can be placed anywhere across the page to help align objects; some programs will let you convert any path into a guide to make things easier.

Snapping options can make points snap to the grid, guides, or each other. As you move the mouse—whether getting ready to make a new point or dragging an existing point or object—the pointer will jump onto any snapping object it passes near. This makes it easier to ensure that shapes are precisely overlaid or butted up to each other. Some drawing programs go a step further, offering smart guides that pop up to let you know when lines are parallel with others or at a specified angle.

4. Click where you want the fourth point, and keep the mouse button held while you drag out a curve, as before.

5. Click and let go of the final point to complete the arches. In this example, we kept the handles aligned horizontally by holding down the Shift key.

## Bézier curves 2. Shapes and switchbacks

Continuing a curve through the line formed by a pair of handles makes an S- shape. Doubling back from a corner makes a pointed shape.

1. This time we'll draw a curly bracket. Having made the first point, click the second, and hold the mouse button.

2. Now drag out the handles to form a curve. So far, the shape is the same as in step 2 of the previous example.

3. This time, place the third point higher up. Click and let go to make a corner. The curve forms an S-shape.

## Bézier curves 3. Bulges and forced corners

This cloud shape relies on the basic Bézier principles: click for a corner, drag for a curve. But some extra tricks are required.

1. Having clicked to make the first point, click where you want the second and let go, forming a corner.

2. Click the third point and drag to make a bulge without an extra point (a parabola). Continuing the curve upward would make an S-shape . . .

3. . . . but we want to double back. So, still holding the mouse button, press the Option key to move only one handle, and drag it back to the point.

## Bézier curves 4. Editing Bézier paths

Every point and handle doesn't have to be right first time. Various ways of editing paths are common to most drawing programs.

1. Points can be moved using a Selection tool. Holding the Shift key lets you select several points, which can then be moved all at once.

2. Using the same tool, you can move handles. One handle of a pair can be moved to a different distance, although always remaining parallel.

DIGITAL DRAWING

4. Click and drag the fourth point to make
a second curve symmetrical with the first.

5. Click and let go of the final point to complete the bracket.
Using basic principles, we have made a more complex shape.

4. This lets you make a corner. Click where you want
the fourth point, and drag to make an ordinary curve.

5. After clicking to make the fifth point a corner, click back on
the first point to complete the closed path and drag out a bulge.

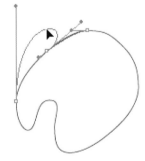

3. Clicking a point with a Convert tool
retracts its handles, making it a corner.
The same tool can drag handles in
non-parallel directions.

4. Dragging from a point with the Convert
tool replaces its handles with a new pair,
in a symmetrical and parallel relationship.

5. In some programs, you can drag the curves
themselves to reshape them; surrounding
points' handles are automatically adjusted.

**EVERY VECTOR PATH** has a "stroke" and "fill," and changing these properties can transform simple lines into vibrant artwork. The stroke governs the appearance of the path itself; it may be invisible (no stroke), or may appear as a line of given thickness and color. When a path is closed, the space it encloses can also be filled with a chosen color or pattern.

# Stroke and fill

Basic strokes consist of a single line. The thickness of each—also known as the line weight—is usually measured in points, as with typeface size, although you can specify it in other units such as millimeters if you prefer. Colors can be selected from predefined libraries supplied with your software, picked from a color wheel, or specified using sliders based on CMYK, RGB, or other color models (see pages 188–191). You can also store colors as swatches for future use.

Various dotted or dashed strokes can be selected, and special line ends can be applied in shapes such as arrowheads. More complex strokes can be applied using brushes; this is explored in further detail on pages 92–95.

1. It is easiest to draw shapes with a fine stroke, such as 0.25 pt.

Basic

0c45m91... ↔ 6

Overprint  Miter limit: 4

Cap: ⬛ ⬜ ⬜  Join: ⬕ ⬕ ⬕

No dash

2. Any desired thickness and color can be applied to strokes in the finished artwork.

Basic

0c 45m 90. ↔ 6

Overprint  Miter: 4

Cap: ⬛ ⬜ ⬜  Join: ⬕ ⬕ ⬕

3. Most programs offer a variety of dotted and dashed strokes, often customizable by the user.

Brush

Zig Pattern 1  Options

↔ 200 %

4. Brush tools can be used to apply complex strokes or arrange small objects along a path.

# Fills

Basic fills can be applied by choosing a color. Gradient fills blend smoothly from one color to another within an object, creating subtler shading. A linear gradient sweeps from side to side at a given angle, while a radial gradient progresses from one color at a center point to another at the edge. Almost all vector programs now support multipoint gradients, which can pass through any number of points between beginning and end; colors are added as points on a bar representing the whole gradient. Some packages offer additional types of gradients. Shapes can also be filled with patterns, which you can define yourself by creating smaller objects that are automatically tiled to fill the required space. Finally, any vector artwork, or an imported bitmap image, can be placed within a shape to fill it. This is known as a "clipping" mask.

However, almost all types of fill have the same limitation in common: although they are clipped by the edges of any objects that they are applied to, they do not distort to match its shape. A radial fill, for example, always progresses in concentric circles, whether or not the object it is filling is circular. Realistic shading can be created manually using the Blend command, which constructs intermediate stages between two or more shapes (see page 84).

Alternatively, Illustrator's Gradient Fill feature creates a kind of fill mesh that can have different colors dropped into different areas and be reshaped at will.

1. The Expand feature can turn strokes into outlines that recreate the stroke widths.

2. An expanded stroke object can be given its own fill and stroke settings, creating a double outline.

DIGITAL DRAWING

3. Illustrator's Gradient Mesh turns simple shapes into meshes ready for complex coloring.

4. Click or drop colors onto the mesh and manipulate the points of the mesh itself to produce complex airbrush-like effects.

Left: This complex illustration has been meticulously constructed using a wide range of fills and strokes, including plain and dashed strokes, simple fills, gradients, and complex fills created by blending between objects. The result is almost photorealistic, but with a precision and consistency that could only be achieved in vector drawing.

PICTURE: TREVOR JOHNSTON FOR MACROMEDIA

# Fills

**Fills**

1. A basic fill consists of a single color. This fills the shape without overlapping the stroke.

2. Here, we have applied a simple two-color linear gradient.

3. For a richer effect, we have used a radial fill and added colors to the gradient bar.

4. Here, we have turned a gradient-filled circle into a tile, which is automatically repeated to fill the shape.

DIGITAL DRAWING

**Advanced fills**

1. To make a hole in a shape, draw one path within another, and make them into a compound path (use the Pathfinder panel in Illustrator).

2. Here, we have applied a radial gradient to several objects, then changed the colors contained in each.

3. To place color more like an airbrush, use the Gradient Mesh and manipulate the mesh lines.

4. Any shape can also contain an image. In Illustrator, place the shape over the image, select them both, then choose Compound Path from the Object menu.

**THE CONCEPT OF LAYERED ELEMENTS** is fundamental to vector drawing. Every object you draw has a place in the stacking order—when shapes overlap, it is the stacking order that dictates which appear in front of the others. By default, each new object you draw is placed at the top of the stack, and appears in front of others.

# Stacking and layers

You will often need to rearrange objects as you work, and this is possible using the commands Send to Back, Send to Front, Send Backward, and Send Forward. The latter two swap an object with the previous or following one in the stacking order, and can be repeated until the order is right.

As an object moves down the stacking order, it can disappear behind others. In Illustrator, if you know it is there you can try selecting it using the Next Object Below command in the Select menu. Alternatively, switch to Outline view in the View menu to see everything in wireframe skeleton form, select the shape you want, then switch back to the Preview view mode.

If you group a number of objects together so that they are moved and scaled as one, the group occupies a single place in the stacking order. The objects maintain their stacking relationship with each other, but cannot be moved individually in front or behind others outside the group.

In complex illustrations, the number of objects and groups can be very large, and it can be hard to manage their stacking order. To help, you can use "layers." As in bitmap programs, these work like transparent sheets on which you place elements; those underneath show through in empty areas. Layers themselves can then be put in a stacking order, and moved forward or backward by clicking and dragging their names

Some vector programs show a nested list of layers, groups, and objects, which clarifies the stacking order.

The transparency and blending mode of each object can be defined.

within a list. In some programs, objects and groups are also shown, giving a complete breakdown of the stacking order of the artwork, and letting objects be selected without having to find and click on them directly.

Top row:
1. A hand is drawn, and appears as the first object in the stacking order.
2. Three stars are drawn. Since they'll want to remain together, we have grouped them.
3. A banknote shape is drawn. Being the most recent object, it appears on top, covering the other elements.

4. The banknote is sent to the back. This places it lowest in the stacking order, behind the other objects and at the bottom of the list.
5. A shape is drawn on a new layer. Although it is at the top within this layer, it underlies the other elements, as its layer is lower than theirs.

Bottom row:
1. The Blending mode of the hand is changed from Normal to Multiply. Its color now combines with that of underlying objects.
2. The Blending mode of the banknote is changed to Color Burn. Only the background shape is affected; the others are on top.
3. The banknote is brought to the front. The colors of the hand and

stars are now modified where the banknote intersects.
4. A white stroke is added to the banknote which is in Color Burn mode. White is neutral in this mode, so the stroke isn't seen.
5. Instead, to make a visible outline, a copy of the banknote is pasted on top. This is given a white stroke, no fill, and then Blending mode is set at Normal.

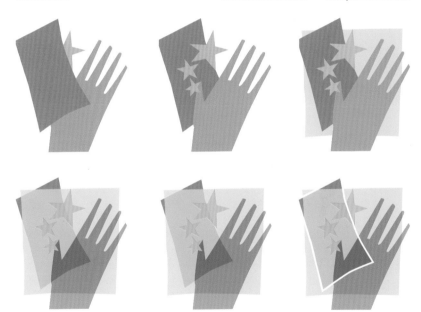

An increasing number of vector applications let objects be "transparent." In this case, underlying objects show through to a specified extent. Stacking principles are preserved and underlying objects or layers never modify those above. Since output devices, including those of commercial printers, may not support transparency functions, artwork can be exported with transparent elements by either being converted to intersected vector objects or to high-resolution bitmaps.

**VECTOR ILLUSTRATIONS** commonly employ a variety of techniques. The illustration here uses several different ways of adding shading effects, as the pulled-out graphics demonstrate. The cone of the blue building on page 89 is shaded by drawing a dark outline (the body of the cone) and a brighter highlight (the light streak running down the left side). Blending these two elements together creates a smooth graduation between the dark and light.

# Exploded drawing

The roof of the brown building in the center of the image has been created by filling flat elements with a graduated color. Although easier to handle than blends, gradient fills can only be either linear or circular, and so need to be used with care. Although the same gradient was applied to every element in this roof, the directions of the gradients were altered each time in order to give an impression of roundness.

The superhero figure was initially filled with flat colors. Illustrator's Gradient Mesh feature (see page 128) lets spots of other colors be placed by simply choosing the color and clicking

Below:
1. The basic outline of the superhero figure is drawn overa scanned template.
2. Each element of the outline is filled with solid colors as appropriate.
3. Black, stylized shadows are drawn straight onto the figure. Here they have been separated to show them in isolation.
4. The color figure, together with its shadows.

5. A paler version of the main costume color is placed as a Gradient Mesh into the solid color, creating a soft blend effect.
6. Because Illustrator objects do not support both the Gradient Mesh feature and stroke on a single object, a new unfilled stroke has to be prepared to provide an outline for the figure.
7. The completed figure, with Gradient Mesh and stroke.

DIGITAL DRAWING

This illustration gives an idea of the processes involved in building a complex piece of artwork. The tear-away beneath the main, shaded illustration shows the individual paths alone, without any fill. Beneath that, the tear-away shows the type of scanned rough drawing frequently used as a template. The digital illustration can be drawn on top of this.

Above: The dome of this building comprises just five separate elements. When overlaid on top of each other and filled with a simple gradient, they create a convincing illusion of 3D.

# Exploded drawing

at an appropriate point; the two colors are blended together automatically, producing a pleasing airbrush effect.

Because this image uses isometric projection rather than true perspective (see page 110), drawing the buildings themselves was a simple matter. In each case, a single window was drawn, matching the perspective of the building. The window was then duplicated horizontally as many times as required, and the group of windows was duplicated vertically until they filled the face of the building. One building was duplicated and re-colored to make several others; windows were re-colored at random to give the impression of lights behind them. The windows on the circular building are a special case (see the opposite page to find out how this was done).

Above: The dome of the tower is made of three elements: the front and side of the dome itself, and the spike on top. Smaller versions of the spike and front are filled with a paler color and positioned to create a blend focus. Ten steps are created between the beginning and end of the main blend; here they are spread out so we can see each one. The spike uses just three intermediate steps. The completed dome, with all the blend stages in their correct position.

Right: 1. The outline is created by drawing an arc, duplicating it, then joining the endpoints and filling with a gradient.
2. A shorter version of the resulting shape is filled with solid yellow for the window band.
3. Vertical bars are drawn on top of this single window to mark the dividing sections of the windows.
4. Illustrator's Pathfinder palette allows us to subtract the vertical bars from the band, turning it into a ring of individual windows.
5. By repeating steps 2–4, more windows can be created with ease.

DIGITAL DRAWING

1. The elements of the tower are drawn as individual objects. A single blue ring is drawn and then scaled toward the apex of the tower; this operation was duplicated to make the rest of the rings.

2. A dark triangle forms the basis of the cone, while a smaller, lighter colored triangle is used for the highlight. The two are then blended together to create the final shading effect seen here.

3. The vapor trail from the rocket is drawn and filled with a solid color, then placed on top of the tower. The opacity of this vapor trail is reduced to 80% to let the tower underneath show through.

# DRAWING TECHNIQUES

**3**

**THE APPLICATIONS** Adobe Illustrator and CorelDRAW have given digital illustrators more artistic freedom with features that allow the illustrator to stretch beyond the basics of vector drawing, and introduce more "natural media" effects.

So far we have covered the most fundamental aspects of vector drawing, and the results are impressive already. But we have only just scratched the surface. The two main applications on the market—Illustrator and CorelDRAW— now come with a range of features that give you additional artistic scope. You can give an outline a rough-sketched look with one click, then an artistic watercolor style with another. Calligraphic, Pattern, and Scatter brushes enable you to turn basic paths into something quite spectacular, and as these brushes adhere to the vector path beneath, changing the length, angle, or style of a stroke can be done with ease. You can also use the Gradient Mesh tool to simulate realistic 3D shading, or use a "mesh" to distort simple objects into strange and wonderful new shapes. It is even possible to convert a bitmap image, such as a photograph, into the paths, strokes, and fills of a vector graphic, creating almost instant drawings.

The strengths of the object-centered approach also make vector-based applications a natural choice for those tasks that can make up the bulk of a working illustrator's job. Isometric and technical drawings are straightforward, maps can be made with a minimum of worry, while the ability to copy and repurpose objects can save huge amounts of time. An architect or engineer would use more specialized software to design an office building or complex mechanism, but vector-based packages use similar techniques and can give your image the same clean, scientific look.

Opposite: Created using a range of Illustrator's Art Brushes, this digital illustration emulates the look of natural media brush strokes.

**ADOBE ILLUSTRATOR'S ART BRUSHES** are drawings of typical brush strokes that can be wrapped around the stroke lines of artwork.

# Brushes

They have the ability to make the simplest line drawings look like complex creations, and have the added advantage that the underlying artwork can be edited as easily as if the Art Brushes hadn't been applied to them. Brushes can be resized, re-colored, and tweaked endlessly to suit the job in hand, either globally or individually for each group or stroke.

When an Art Brush is applied to base artwork, it acts on top of the underlying structure without altering it. This makes it easy to try out a variety of different strokes to see which one best suits the illustration. You commit yourself irrevocably to the effect only if you specifically choose to do so, at which point the strokes are turned into regular Illustrator outlines, ready to be adjusted just like any other artwork. This system offers tremendous flexibility and scope for experimentation, without creating over-complex artwork that would be hard to edit.

Art Brush strokes are stretched to fit the entire length of a selected path. In practice, this can make the stroke look artificial and unwieldy, but there is a way around this. As our example on the opposite page shows, breaking that path into several smaller paths forces the Art Brush stroke to redraw itself for each path segment, resulting in a more flowing and natural appearance.

Custom brushes can do far more than simulating natural media. Any object drawn in Illustrator can be defined as a brush. Along with Art Brushes, which follow a drawn stroke, there are also Scatter Brushes (which place multiple instances of the artwork along the stroke), Calligraphic Brushes (which place an angled line along the stroke), and Pattern Brushes (useful for creating custom borders). Each comes with its own range of variations—so that Scatter Brushes, for example, can be set to vary in size, spacing, rotation, and scattering from the drawn path.

Left: Dozens of useful custom Art Brushes are available for you to browse through. You can also create your own.

Bottom row: 1. This simple outline drawing is the basis for our brush stroke. The drawing is unfilled, and the stroke lines are kept relatively short.
2. The Charcoal brush adds roughness and complexity to the outline, with a suitably scratchy appearance.
3. The Fountain Pen brush is smoother in feel, but it is still a distinctly leaky pen.

4. The Watercolor brush uses multiple shades of gray to create a soft, almost transparent look.
5. The Watercolor brush again, this time colored in shades of red and yellow—the stroke size has been increased for a less-controlled look.
6. The same Watercolor brush, but now with a copy of the artwork placed on top using the Fountain Pen brush at an opacity of 75%.

# Brushes

Left: 1. This simple outline of a hand will be the basis for our Art Brush application.
2. When the Art Brush is applied to the hand, the single brush stroke follows the outline from beginning to end.
Left bottom: 3. We can divide this single path into several smaller ones by cutting it at the points shown.
4. Now, each application of the Art Brush fits just that segment of the outline, resulting in a more natural look.

Right and opposite: The two elements used in this image—a blade of grass and a bubble—are defined as two custom brushes: the grass as an Art brush, the bubble as a Scatter brush.
Opposite top left: Several strokes are drawn, using the Grass brush. By changing the color of each stroke, we can vary the appearance.
Opposite top right: Another layer of brushstrokes has its opacity lowered to make it recede into the distance.
Opposite bottom: By setting random scaling, spacing, and scatter, we can make the bubbles follow a few drawn paths in a natural manner.

DIGITAL DRAWING

**CEL SHADING** refers to the style of using flat block colors to represent areas of light and shadow on a picture.

# Line, color, and tone

The use of darker and lighter tones to define shape and shadow is intrinsic to most forms of illustration. One of the simplest forms is cel-style shading that originates from early animation where cells were used to build up each frame: it is very easy to emulate using Adobe Photoshop. By making the most of layers, it is possible to achieve a high-quality look very quickly. The time can be spent focusing on the details rather than getting the overall cel look to work effectively.

Finally, cel shading is often the basis for many other visual styles, such as airbrush or natural media, and acts as the basis of lighting for most images. Time spent on the cel shading process will improve the look of any image, regardless of the look you require for the final piece.

The lightest parts of an object are those that face the light source, and the darkest parts are those that face away from the light. Unless the light source is very small and weak (such as the glow from a TV screen or a flickering flame) the light will affect the object equally. In other words, about the same amount of light falls on all the areas that point toward the light. The light source on this pig (bottom right) is originating from the top left, so any areas facing away from there have been shaded more darkly.

DIGITAL DRAWING

Above: Effective definition of shadows can make all the difference to how "solid" your picture looks. When the objects in the scene are obviously affecting one another, your picture becomes much more believable. Firstly, the pig now casts a shadow onto the floor. The shape of his body has been defined, and the ears can be seen in the shadow too. Secondly, the pig is also casting shadows on himself. You can see how the snout is blocking the light from his face and the two legs nearest us are not directly lit at all. It's easy for objects to cast shadows on themselves, so you need to be aware of this.

Above: With shiny materials such as plastic or skin (in some instances), you may wish to further define the shadows. Giving these areas a heavier shadow can help to define the shape of the object more vividly.

Below: Highlights are only necessary on shiny materials, and can be used to a greater or lesser degree depending on the effect that is desired. In this image, highlights have been added from the main light source. However, some additional highlights have been added in the opposite direction, implying some sort of other light source nearby. This style of "backlight" is quite a popular method to give an object more volume.

# Line, color, and tone

Left: Prepare an image for cel shading by making sure it has the base colors applied.

Above: A medium-range color, such as a mid blue or a dull pink is used for the shadows. Gray is an alternative too, but will generally come out more drab than a tinted shade. In any case, this color can be easily changed later, so it doesn't matter too much at this stage. Using the Brush tool with a hard-edged brush, color is applied roughly over the image in the areas away from the light source.

Below: Using either the Eraser tool or the Brush tool set to white, the shadows can be cleaned up, and definition added to the shading.

Below: By revealing the color layer, you can now choose how to adjust your colors. You can easily work on shading with the colors turned on.

Left: The brightest highlights are added to shiny areas such as the metal pins and hair. Keeping the color white, more highlights are added as small dots, lines, and "glints" of white light to areas which would especially pick up the light.

Below: With all the layers visible, the shaded image in its completed form.

**CHARACTER DESIGN** is essential to effective visual storytelling and creating digital cartoons. The digital medium offers a huge range of different style treatments that can be used for characters.

# Cartoons

Cartoons are amongst the oldest form of artistic expression and are predated only by verbal storytelling. From the first daubings on a cave wall to the wonders of Disney and Pixar, visual storytelling has now found a new home as a digital medium. Character design is at the heart of all cartoons and comic strips. Essentially if you create good characters with convincing motives and put them in a situation together the stories will create themselves

A whole cast ready for action.

DIGITAL DRAWING

One character, ten different treatments.

# Cartoons

## What to look for

Emotion. Themes such as love, hate, and jealousy should ultimately drive your characters and create the plot.

Humor. It is not always appropriate, but even in the darkest tales, humor can enrich the writing.

Layers of story. Don't overdo it, but you can run concurrent stories, either in the picture, dialogue, or background.

Layers of meaning. Embedding extra themes and motives shows the complexity of life.

Stay focused. It is easy to wander off the main plot and go down blind alleys. Put every idea through a simple test: Does it help the story or not?

Structure. Build a strong plot structure. Once it is in place, you can hang all kinds of embellishments and details on it and the story will still work.

Rhythm. A good story will take you through fast and slow parts. Even an action comic needs quiet moments to allow readers to catch their breath.

Incidentals. Sometimes it is worth focusing on a detail, an object, something that someone said, or a view from a window. Details can add richness and texture to a story.

Establishing scene. It is traditional in film and television that if you change scenes you should have a general shot showing where the action is taking place and the positions of the characters. This also applies to comics.

Villains (the interesting ones). Villains should have some depth—a reason for their hatred. Some of the best ones are not evil at all; they just have a different point of view.

Subtlety. Many actions and emotions are best described with subtle visual gestures, such as a look or a posture.

## What to avoid

Too much text. Characters giving long speeches, especially if they are just giving an exposition of the plot, soon lose the reader's attention.

Villains (the boring ones). Try to avoid cardboard cutouts, or evil guys with one thing on their mind, particularly "world domination."

Inconsistent motives. Characters should change their motives only with events that affect them, not just to suit the plot.

Too much atmosphere. Endless frames filled with gloomy landscapes are tedious and wasteful of a comic buyer's hard-earned money. Atmosphere is a visual thing that can be carried behind the action, apart from the odd establishing shot.

Overbearing plot. Overly complex plots are never a substitute for good storytelling. Find the appropriate level for your story and audience, then stick to it.

Talking heads. Readers tend to get bored by too much dialogue because it is visually static. If you have a dialogue-rich section, keep it interesting by including secondary visual action in the frame.

**SOONER OR LATER,** every digital artist is asked to create a map. The quality of the end result depends on your artistic inspiration, but by bearing some basic rules in mind you can take much of the tedium out of the process. The basic technique is simple. Begin by drawing a network of roads, either freehand or by tracing over a sketch.

# Maps and plans

While it's possible to use an existing map as a guide, this should be done with extreme caution: copyright in maps is heavily protected, and using someone's design can mean serious trouble.

Roads should be drawn using a thick black stroke (the width of the line) with no fill. The thickness can depend on the importance of each road, if you wish—but it is important to draw each road as a separate path to make editing easier later. Once all the roads are drawn, there's a useful trick for the outlines. First, duplicate the road layer. Then lock the original so that it will not be accidentally altered. Now change the color of the stroke on the copy to a light color (white or yellow work well), and reduce the stroke width. This lets the underlying road show through, and creates an outline. The smaller the new stroke, the thicker the outlines—so, if the roads use a 9-pt stroke, and the copy uses a 7-pt stroke, the new roads will be 2-pt smaller, resulting in a 1-pt stroke on both edges. Try to vary this for major and minor roads.

There are several ways of creating other "line" elements, such as rivers and railway lines. To draw a river of uniform thickness, a custom brush made up of parallel blue lines on a pale blue background can be created. When applied to a stroke, this will make a stylized river similar to those on underground maps. For a more realistic

Opposite: 1. Begin by drawing the roads that define your map. Set your roads to have a black stroke, but no fill. Draw each road as a separate path.

2. Now increase the stroke for your roads as appropriate. The minor roads here have been given a 9-pt stroke, while the major roads have a thicker 15-pt stroke.

3. Now duplicate the road layer to make an exact copy of it, and change the stroke on the new layer to a contrasting color. By reducing the stroke width, we make outlines for each road: a 7-pt yellow stroke provides a 1-pt outline for the minor roads, and an 11-pt stroke makes a 2-pt outline for the major roads.

4. Duplicate the road layer again, and cut the path into segments where each name will appear; the Text on a Path feature will let the names run along the roads perfectly.

5. The parkland is drawn on a new layer behind the road layers. It isn't necessary to follow the original road lines exactly, as the roads themselves will cover any discrepancies. This is also a good time to choose a background color. Pick one that contrasts strongly with the map data.

6. The river and railways are drawn using different kinds of stroke— an Art Brush for the river, and a simple dashed stroke for the rails.

7. After the place names have been added (on their own layer), duplicate the layer and add a white stroke to make them stand out.

8. With the data in place, it is time to start tinkering. Adding a drop shadow by duplicating a road layer makes them stand out: coloring the major roads differently is simply a matter of changing their stroke color. Finally, we can add variations in the background tone by using a Gradient Mesh, although this can be hard to control —a white mask as the top covers the ragged edges.

approach, you will have to draw the river varying in thickness and simply fill it with a pale blue.

You can create custom brushes for railway lines, but there's an easier way. First, draw your rail using a thin black stroke with no fill. Then duplicate this path, and apply a dashed stroke to it: this alternates solid with empty spaces along the path. By increasing the stroke width, and inserting large spaces as the gaps between the dashes, it is easy to simulate a railway line.

# Maps and plans

Left: In this map, too, the content is restricted to relevant subject matter. The underlying tonal base, indicating topographic structure, enhances the simple treatment of the other items.

YEOVIL

B3146

Cross
in
Hand

Lyons
Gate

Evershot

Beaminster
Down

East
Hill

B3143

A356

Cerne
Abbas

Beaminster

A352

BRIDPORT

A35

Roman Road

DORCHESTER

miles 1   2   3   4   5

km   2   4   6   8

Above: Sometimes you will need to show information at local area level together with a wider overview. Rather than attempting to show the detail on a single map, you could use two or more maps with different scales. At each level, the next stage map is shown as an inset area. Varying the size of the map, with the biggest map being the main focus, creates an interesting arrangement.

For a more dynamic effect, you can rotate and angle the maps.

# Maps and plans

DIGITAL DRAWING

Opposite and below: It is not always necessary for the illustrator to create maps from scratch. There are resources available that enable you to edit and adapt pre-configured maps saving much time and effort: prominent amongst these is Mountain High Maps Plus. The text is editable and is supplied as a kit of Illustrator files, one for each map. To these are added both land and ocean floor relief as high resolution bitmap files in TIFF and JPEG formats. Features like political boundaries rivers and masks for various regions can be turned on or off making it possible to create a limitless number of visual options using either Illustrator, Photoshop, or even InDesign. The world maps can also be wrapped round a sphere using the 3D features now available in Photoshop.

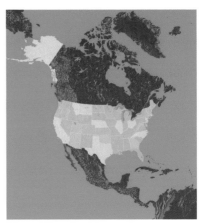

**ISOMETRIC DRAWING** is a form of perspective whereby horizontal lines are converted to 30° angles, in both directions. Unlike real perspective illustrations, there's no vanishing point, so objects do not diminish with distance. It is a style favored by technical illustrators for its combination of ease of drawing and clarity of appearance.

# Isometric drawing

Exploded diagrams of computer innards, engine parts, and electrical components generally use isometric drawings in order to show clearly and precisely how the elements fit together. A number of non-technical illustrators have also adopted the form to create arresting, heavily stylized images.

Isometric projection is also a favorite with game designers (although they generally work in a bitmap rather than vector environment).

Games such as Sim City, which need to display a large number of buildings, roads, and natural features, incorporate this drawing method because the lack of true perspective simplifies the visual style and enables the game to run more smoothly.

Creating an isometric grid is one way to draw using this projection: snapping each pen point to a grid line will ensure that, with a little thought,

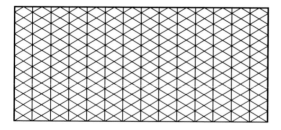

Left: If you are creating drawings from scratch, it can help to make an isometric grid such as this one. Begin with an array of vertical lines, then group and skew them 60° to make one dimension axis—copy and flip the result horizontally to make the other axis.

Left: In isometric drawings, each dimension retains its natural size. So although the sides of this cube appear to be going back in perspective, the length of each side still measures the same.

DIGITAL DRAWING

As well as drawing isometric projections from scratch, it is also possible to turn existing artwork into an isometric view. Here, we'll begin with this head-on view of an old radio.

Above right: The first step is to scale the artwork horizontally by 86.6% (the cosine of 30°), and then shear it vertically 30°. This makes the first isometric plane.

Top right: The side and top are added by duplicating the back layer, cutting the path, then offsetting a duplicate of the cut path and joining the endpoints together. Filled with just the standard brown, it looks rather dull.

Right: A Gradient fill, set to the same 30°, is designed to provide a dark side with a highlight on the rounded corner. The knobs are given depth by simply duplicating them, the aerial is made from a copy of the knob, and a bevel on the inside of the speaker grille adds a sense of depth.

Illustrator's Smart Guides feature enables pen paths and movements to snap to 30° alignments with existing points in the artwork, making it an ideal tool for creating isometric drawings.

you follow the correct angles. This is the way a traditional illustrator would work, and this method has its application here as well. But in the digital arena, we have more powerful tools at our disposal: specifically, the ability to shear artwork (skewing it along a single axis) by a

precise 30°, as well as the ability to scale artwork by 86.6%. This is the cosine of 30°, and is the angle required to make "side" faces appear in the correct proportions. The example above shows how to create an isometric view from existing artwork using these two techniques.

# Isometric drawing

Above: Still keeping the detail minimal, and the treatment mostly line and flat tone, this image uses a ghosting technique and arrows to illustrate a simple process. It also is drawn to a regular 30° projection, which makes it simpler to construct using a 2D vector program.

Left: A diagram like this is relatively simple to construct digitally in line and color. The image is drawn on a 30° projection. It has some basic tone work and graduated tints to give a 3D effect. Arrows are used to indicate potential movement of parts of the object.

**TECHNICAL DRAWING** is not a field every illustrator would wish to stray into, but it is an important category in its own right. Technical illustrations generally use an isometric projection of the type described on the previous pages, which provides a clear view of how different components fit together.

# Technical drawing

The trick in drawing diagrams of this kind is to repurpose picture elements wherever possible. Since vector programs enable artwork to be scaled, rotated, and manipulated with no loss of quality whatsoever, the individual parts can be drawn to any size and then scaled as required.

The examples on these pages use a gradient fill to add texture to the illustrations; by applying a common gradient to all the elements of the illustration, a homogeneous appearance can be achieved. It is then possible to change the gradient globally at a later date, or even remove it entirely—a lot of technical drawing relies on white fills with simple black outlines for clarity.

Crosshatching—drawing an array of parallel lines to simulate shading—is a useful technique for adding depth to line artwork. Adobe Illustrator has a complex crosshatching engine that can apply a variety of styles of hatching with a high level of user control.

Below:
1. To create a 3D cogwheel, begin by drawing a circle.
2. The first tooth is drawn by radiating two lines from the center of the circle, then joining them together at the ends.
3. This tooth is rotated 30°, and the operation is duplicated to make the rest of the teeth.
4. All the elements are merged into one, and a central, smaller circle is knocked out from the whole assembly.
5. The flat cog is compressed horizontally, and duplicated to make the thickness of the cog.
6. Each face of each tooth is drawn as a new element to add solidity to the wheel.
7. A simple gradient shading makes the wheel look more 3D.

Above: Multiple copies of the cylinder can be scaled, stretched, and combined to form a wide variety of shapes.

Above: When the simple gradient is changed to a more complex one, the cylinder stack begins to look far more metallic.

# Technical drawing

Line

Delineated line

Line and tone

Above: Three commonly used methods of technical drawing

Right: There are several methods of illustrating elements that would normally be obscured in a straightforward illustration. The cutaway removes obscuring parts.

DIGITAL DRAWING

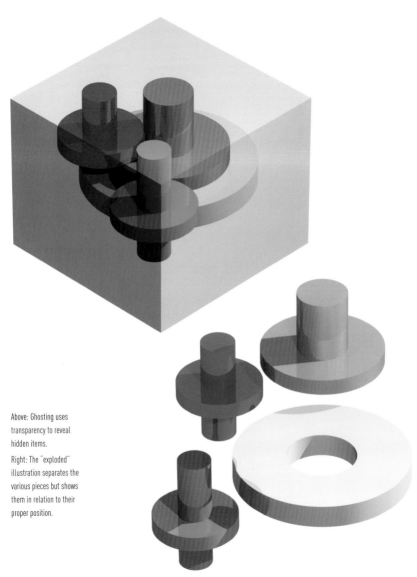

Above: Ghosting uses transparency to reveal hidden items.

Right: The "exploded" illustration separates the various pieces but shows them in relation to their proper position.

# Illustrative diagrams

With so many possible variations of style, structure and levels of complexity, illustrative diagrams share one thing in common: they have to communicate a message. They can be used to create a visual language substituting effectively for words, and transcend normal language barriers. Sensible color application gives them even greater scope. The use of common angles, line weights, and color helps to create clarity and avoid ambiguity.

Left and opposite: Illustrative diagrams are often used in sequence, breaking down a complex activity into a series of simple steps. Make sure the steps have enough common elements, so that the series flows visually. Label each stage clearly and make sure that the parts for each are separated enough, so that parts don't get confused. In this example, size remains constant up to stage six, when it is enlarged for clarity. Arrows are used to illustrate movement, and their function is explained in a key. Letters are used to orientate the reader, and these are distinguished from the sequence numbers by color. Note also the subtle use of shading to indicate variations in the planes of surfaces. The sequence is completed by the photograph of the result.

........... Fold line

Fold

Turn

Pull

# Illustrative diagrams

Opposite: This detailed rendering of a traditional brewing oast house would take some time to draw by any method. Creating it with 3D software gives the designer the flexibility to select the best view for the overall design. It also enables variations of lighting effect to be tried. The image could be incorporated into an animated sequence, and could have the further advantage of being available for reuse (subject to copyright conditions).

Above Diagrammatic illustrations of reality are best left to the competent specialists. Despite the wealth of ingenious digital aids now available, it takes years of experience to construct images that are convincing. Nevertheless, the current software does facilitate the rough planning of designs to a surprising degree of finish and can save hours of preplanning time.

**COMMUNICATING STATISTICS** through diagrams can be done very effectively through pictorial variations on the classic bar chart model.

# Statistical diagrams

**3**

Of all statistical diagrams it is those based on the bar chart that are most suited to a pictorial expression. By placing two or more bars together you can see the absolute vaule of each and the

relative difference between them. They can be arranged vertically or horizontally and they should all have a recognizeable baseline.

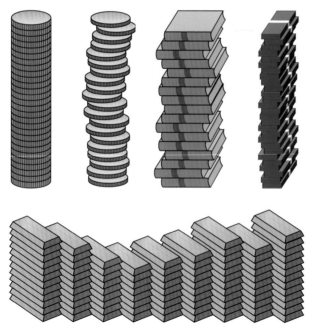

Left and below left: Of course, you can create 3D bars by drawing a series of objects in 3D. Shading also can be used to enhance the visual effect.

DIGITAL DRAWING

Above: A chart like this definitely carries visual impact, and is not so difficult to achieve with currently available software, clip art, and a little imagination. It could be used to represent a whole range of travel-related activities.

Above: Here a familiar object is used as the bar. The cassette is created out of circles and lines, and the film strip is even simpler.

Above: You may want to add character to your charts by using pictorial elements that have a more informal, cartoon-like treatment.

# Statistical diagrams

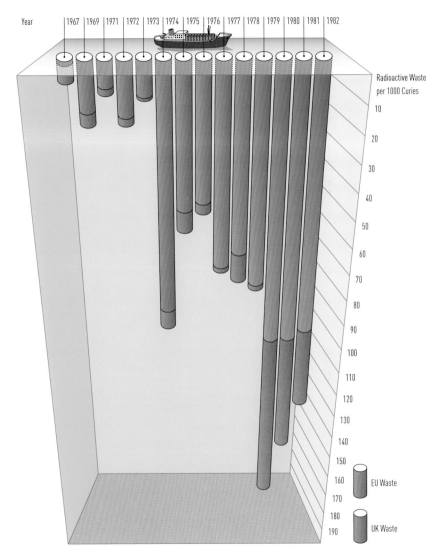

Year | 1967 | 1969 | 1971 | 1972 | 1973 | 1974 | 1975 | 1976 | 1977 | 1978 | 1979 | 1980 | 1981 | 1982

Radioactive Waste
per 1000 Curies

10
20
30
40
50
60
70
80
90
100
110
120
130
140
150
160
170
180
190

EU Waste

UK Waste

**TRACING AND AUTOTRACING** Given the existence of both bitmap and vector applications and images, it is inevitable that artwork will need to be converted between the two. There are a number of ways to do this, each with advantages and disadvantages. While sometimes it is best to do things manually, most drawing packages have an easier, automatic tracing option.

# Tracing

**3**

One solution is quite straightforward: each pixel can simply be replaced by a geometric square filled with the same color. In practice, however, this would be both pointless and massively inefficient. The challenge is to transform bitmap imagery into something representing the same subject, but with the distinctive economy (both aesthetic and technical) of vector art.

At the academic end of the software development industry, many different methods of applying vectors to bitmap artwork have been explored and incorporated into specialized programs. Converting a bitmap into vector shapes is known as autotracing—in Adobe Illustrator this can be carried out with the Live

Trace feature. This offers comprehensive control over the process and can give excellent results, whether you want a clean reproduction of a piece of line art, or a detailed facsimile of a photo. Many artists prefer to draw initial sketches on paper, and Illustrator enables them to scan these and convert them to vectors to form the basis of a resolution-independent illustration.

What this kind of feature cannot do, however, is interpret a photographic image aesthetically, and create a drawing of it in the same way as an artist, or even a child. Although the software can use edge-finding techniques to try to follow the outlines of objects in a scene, it doesn't understand the visual content of the image, and cannot interpret it intelligently.

This is where manual tracing takes over. Trace art has become a genre of digital illustration in its own right and is usually produced without any automation. Instead, after obtaining one or more suitable source images—often by arranging objects or friends into the desired scene, or by taking a digital camera picture—the illustrator loads them into a vector program and draws

Left: Because its subject is clichéd, this image has the visual quality of a pictogram. Technically, however, it is a bitmap containing millions of differently colored pixels. How can we convert it into vector objects?

Left: Illustrator's Live Trace tool looks for one shape at a time. The method is to click near the edge of an object to make the software trace around it. Repeat the process to complete enough objects to make up an image. After considerable trial and error, the end result tends to look something like this. Fills have been added manually, since colors in the image are ignored. This highly stylized drawing could most kindly be described as reminiscent of the original.

Right: Live Trace is assisted by pre-processing the image in Photoshop. Here, we have reduced the number of color levels using Posterize, then removed noise using the Median filter. Tracing flat colors would be easier, but the quality is limited before you start. Only limited control is offered over the tool's operation, so results are hard to improve or customize.

Bézier curves over the top, finally deleting the bitmaps. Any of the usual stroke-and-fill options can be exploited to create a particular look and feel. Styles can range from highly abstract, with just a few lines judiciously used to suggest forms in a 3D space, to detailed and painterly, with complex shading sketched in.

Above: Here, we have filled paths using multipoint gradients. Radial fills give the paints a 3D feel. Linear gradients work similarly on the brush, and produce a simple sweep of light across the palette. The palette shape has been duplicated, sent behind, moved slightly, and darkened to give it thickness. Shadow objects set to Multiply darken underlying colors.

**BÉZIER CURVES** are infinitely editable, but moving points and handles to transform a whole object can be difficult and time consuming. Instead, meshes and distortion controls can create unique effects, pulling graphics and text into unusual shapes and colors. Vector software has the ability to scale, rotate, and skew, and this can be done by entering numeric values or by reshaping an enclosing rectangle, called a bounding box.

# Meshes and distortion

More recently, envelope distortion has been added, which lets objects be fitted to an irregular shape. Imagine an envelope as a flat elastic sheet with the object printed on it. By grabbing any part of the sheet and pulling it in any direction, you distort the surface and the object along with it. The uses of envelope distortion are almost limitless: you can squeeze type into shapes for logos, fit labels onto drawings of 3D containers, or just pull objects around for unique, abstract effects.

Within the software, envelopes are constructed from crisscrossing Bézier curves to form a flexible grid or mesh. Some programs prefer not to present this directly to the user, and instead offer a range of envelopes in predefined shapes that cannot be significantly altered. Adobe Illustrator gives direct control over all points in a mesh.

Illustrator alone can also use meshes to distort color rather than shape. A gradient mesh takes exactly the same form as a distortion envelope, but lets colors be applied to its points, smoothly blending neighboring colors across the grid. The effect is unique, and extremely subtle shading can be built up much more quickly and flexibly than by the conventional method of constructing many separate blends, with end results similar to traditional airbrush illustration. Alternatively, more dramatic color shifts can be introduced for wild effects.

On the downside, no tools have yet been developed that assist in placing and coloring mesh points in such a way as to create particular effects, such as contoured edges. Instead, it is up to the user to build up the desired effect by adding, moving, and coloring points. However, since these are treated as ordinary Bézier points, many of the usual editing tools can provide assistance here. For example, you can press Shift + Click to select several points at once, and then move them all together, scale to push shading outward or inward, or rotate for a twirling effect.

When it comes to output, gradient meshes raise even greater problems than transparency, as they are not supported by any current version of PostScript (the graphics language invented by Adobe which is used by most equipment throughout the pre-press chain). In most cases, the most straightforward and satisfactory way to exchange and print illustrations that use such advanced effects is to export the whole file as a large bitmap, enabling the application to rasterize its own vector code rather than ask other products to do so. To preserve the quality of the vector artwork, however, it is vital to set a high resolution and use anti-aliasing. Before committing to such steps, see whether simply exporting your work as a PDF creates something that your printer can handle.

## Gradient Mesh

Adobe Illustrator's Gradient Mesh tool provides a unique way to blend any number of colors within an object.

1. Used on any shape, the Create Gradient Mesh command adds a grid of color points. A lighter tint can automatically be applied to certain points to make a highlight at the center or edge of the shape.

2. A gradient mesh is formed from Bézier curves, and its points and handles can be moved like any others. Here, the points nearest the edges have been selected together and scaled by 120%.

3. An alternative way to build up a gradient mesh is by clicking, using the Mesh tool, to place individual color points. Whichever way the mesh is created, color applied to any point is blended with those around it.

Below: Gradient meshes can be used to build up complex realistic shading, as seen in this illustration. Each petal, leaf, and stem consists of a single mesh containing several dozen color points.
PICTURE: © 2001 ADOBE SYSTEMS INCORPORATED

Envelope distortions usually remain live after being applied to an object, so you can edit the envelope later or remove it to leave the object intact. Some operations cannot be performed on objects governed by envelopes, the most obvious being applying another envelope for further distortion to give you the option of applying an envelope permanently to an object's geometry. Once this is done, the object consists of ordinary paths that form the distorted shape, and can be edited without restriction. However, it cannot easily be returned to its original form.

# 3D ILLUSTRATION

3D MODELING AND RENDERING

3D APPLICATIONS

**4**

# 3D APPLICATIONS

**WHERE BOTH BITMAP AND VECTOR**-based applications have clear analogs in traditional paper-based art, 3D applications are something altogether different. In a 3D application you are building fully 3D models and arranging them within a virtual world.

By adding complex textures and lighting effects you can create something that looks uncannily realistic. In fact, in the early days of 3D imaging, realism was the main concern. However, it was not too long before artists realized that 3D applications could also create stunning fantasy and science-fiction images, not to mention more stylized and exaggerated cartoon effects. The processes can seem complicated to traditional illustrators but, as with vector-based drawing applications, the object-based approach makes it easy to copy, transform, and reuse elements at will, while the photorealistic results speak for themselves.

There have been several attempts at landscape modelers, but few programs have had the instant appeal of Bryce. Both relatively easy to use and sophisticated in its end result, Bryce can create any landscape you can imagine—and many that you cannot.

Beginning with a blank perspective plane, add water, mountain ranges, individual rocks, and cloud layers to build up the scene. A huge range of naturalistic textures can be applied to any object, with dozens of seas, rock formations, and terrain types to choose from. You can even draw your own landscapes using a "height map," where white areas are raised and black areas depressed. A built-in tree lab lets you design and build your own trees and shrubs, which can be positioned and scaled as you wish. A separate sky lab enables you to tweak, adjust, and modify cloud formations, sun and moon positions, and general weather conditions.

Opposite: Using Poser a wide variety of figures can be created by varying the face and body parameters. Here, two versions of the same basic figure have been composited in Photoshop, where the other elements were added.

**BRYCE** falls into the lower end category of 3D modeling applications, but it is an excellent tool for creating backgrounds and artificial landscapes. It enables you to create detailed vistas from scratch, by placing basic shapes or objects in your scene and combining them with textures.

# Bryce

There are no 3D modeling tools as such in Bryce, but by combining the primitive objects you are using as building blocks—spheres, cubes, cylinders, and so on—it is possible to populate your land-scape with buildings, fantasy scientific artifacts, and alien spaceships. The interface is strongly reminiscent of Poser (see pages 138–139), which is no surprise, since they originated in the same sta-

3D ILLUSTRATION

Below: Finished images can be
rendered to any size—the larger they
are, the more detail will be visible.

ble. Although it may look confusing at first, the controls are easy to master and the tools intuitive.

In Bryce, objects (including terrains) appear as wireframe models. By viewing these from dif-

ferent angles, it's possible to align them precisely with one another. The Preview panel at the top left of the screen shows a full textured view of the scene at postage stamp size, so you

Create ▸  **Edit** ▸  Sky&Fog ▸  Talk

Cylinder 7
**32 polygons**
00:00:00.00

Above: The wireframe working
arena means you can see where
all your objects lie—but complex
scenes can quickly look like
a jumble of lines.

can see how effects such as sky and lighting will change the image.

Rendering the final image, however, is a long process that can take several hours for large file sizes. This is due to the complexity of the rendering rather than any software shortfalls—when complex transparent and mirrored objects are themselves reflected in shimmering water, it takes its toll on the rendering engine.

Bryce is used largely for creating backgrounds for illustrations, and works well when combined with objects from Poser or other 3D applications. The ability to add animation to scenes means that you can design a camera to fly through your artificial landscape, producing movies of sometimes astonishing sophistication. However, as rendering times can be minutes or even hours for each frame, you will need plenty of time to get the most out of it.

3D ILLUSTRATION

Above: The rendered view shows all the objects with texture applied. Even a low-resolution rendering such as this can take 20 minutes or more to create.

**POSER** is a human figure modeler that's capable of producing photorealistic images of people to a quality that can be hard to discern from the real thing. Models can be positioned in any pose, and the links between body parts conform to real limbs as they are moved; stretching an arm out, for example, will make the body lurch forward to follow its motion.

# Poser

Poser provides a huge range of parameters to control every aspect of a figure's physiognomy. While the models that come with the program are fairly basic, third-party developers—most notably DAZ 3D, which created the original models—sell a wide range of additional figures that add realism and flexibility. Body weights can vary from emaciated to overweight, from weedy to superheroic, and individual limbs can be tweaked to suit any purpose.

As you might expect, the head gets the most attention. It is possible to create virtually any expression imaginable, by changing the position of the eyes, mouth, nose, eyebrows, and so on. You can also design any type of head you want—from ultra-realistic to alien—by adjusting the dozens of controls that determine the size, position, and shape of every facial element. DAZ 3D's Michael 2 model, for example, has 230 head controls (including 15 eye shapes, eight eyebrow modifiers, and 12 teeth modifiers), and nearly 350 individual controls for adjusting the shape of the body.

Poser models can be viewed as wireframe models, blocky 3D models, or "skinned" people. When the desired pose and body morph have been achieved, a final rendering of the image will use a combination of texture, reflection, transparency, and bump maps to add realistic skin tones to figures that can be created at any size.

Figures can be composited with backgrounds or other elements in a bitmap-editing program such as Adobe Photoshop. It is also possible to create finished artwork directly in Poser, either by placing backgrounds or by populating a scene with props, landscapes, and room settings.

One of Poser's strengths is its ability to generate animations. A custom Walk Designer makes the figures walk in any choosen manner along a path you draw. Mouths can be posed to synchronize with recorded speech by dropping in one of the range of phoneme mouth shapes at the relevant points. By adding occasional eye blinks and making the chest expand and contract over time to simulate breathing, it is possible to create convincing character animations that you can output as finished movies, or composite with other elements in video-editing applications such as Adobe Premiere or Apple's Final Cut Pro.

However, figures rendered in Poser are rarely perfect, and most of the artwork generated will need tidying up in Photoshop to smooth out sharp edges on body outlines, and to fix any glitches that may have crept into the joints, for instance. The examples below (of the woman) show a rendered image before it has been cleaned up, to show the kinds of errors that may creep in.

Above: Begin by positioning your figure as you want it to appear, taking care not to over-bend any limbs because this would cause distortion. Props can be added at the same time. The figure can then be given hair, and you can choose from a range of clothing types to complete the model.

Left: Poser can generate figures in a variety of modeling styles. Shown here, from left to right: Outline, Wireframe, Hidden Line Wireframe, Shaded Wireframe, Block Shaded, Sketch, Texture Preview, and Fully Rendered.

# 3D MODELING AND RENDERING

**FOR WORK** beyond the scope of the applications already mentioned, you will need a full-blown 3D package. Digital illustrators do not need one of the top-of-the-range solutions, which are designed for advanced animation and effects, and are overly complex for stills artists. With an affordable general-purpose package, you can add tools to provide extra features.

Most can interchange 3D data, and combining a number of applications and plug-ins is often better than using a single package, however advanced it is. But, make your choice carefully. Check that the manufacturer releases regular updates, and will let you upgrade to an improved version when available. Look for a sizable base of users, who will exchange tips and fixes as well as encourage development of the product. Plug-ins are of benefit only if plenty are available in a compatible format—a healthy number of plug-ins from third parties, like smaller companies and amateurs, is a good indicator.

The three basic areas of functionality are modeling, rendering, and animation. It is preferable for a program to offer more than one kind of geometry for modeling. Ideally, polygons, NURBS, and subdivision surfaces should all be present, but two of these is acceptable. Most professional 3D packages support animation, but if this is something you are likely to explore, avoid those with limited animation features. Rendering capabilities vary widely, as do speeds; bear in mind that waiting time can be measured in hours. Some programs let you use separate third-party renderers: Autodesk 3ds Max has at least four plug-in renderers.

Professional packages with the features you are likely to need include Newtek LightWave 3D, Maxon Cinema 4D, Autodesk Softimage, Electric Image Animation System, and form•Z from AutoDesSys. At lower prices there are capable programs such as Strata 3D, Pixels3D, Caligari trueSpace, and Cheetah3D. Among the more expensive are Maya and 3ds Max from Autodesk.

LightWave 3D and Cinema 4D are ideal for the illustrator. Both offer excellent modeling capabilities, and very fast, high-quality rendering. LightWave has a huge community of keen users, and a vast library of free and shareware plug-ins. It also supports HDRI rendering, and has an ingenious

Opposite: Daniel Mackie's style recalls Ralph Steadman and Francis Bacon. It's surprising to see such a visceral approach explored in 3D modeling, but the combination of shiny surfaces with exaggerated cartoon features and wild motion blur helps this image to pack a punch.
DANIEL MACKIE
WWW.DANIEL.MACKIE.CO.UK

user interface. Cinema 4D has a flexible interface and is well suited to rendering very large images, it also has a very fast development schedule. It is also comes in a cut-down edition for graphic artists, Cinema 4D Art.

While 3D applications are extremely demanding, almost any current Mac or PC above bargain-basement level will be capable of handling them.

Memory is vital—1 GB of RAM is a bare minimum, 4 GB would be better—and a large hard disk is a necessity. Otherwise the most significant component is the graphics card, which must be OpenGL accelerated. Again, specifications change quickly, so it is wise to check before buying and choose a reputable graphics card toward the top end of the range.

**3D MODELING** is the process of building the object that you will later render to produce a finished image. All 3D programs have a world coordinate system, starting at 0,0,0—the "world center"—and extending away from that point in all directions. The three perpendicular axes are named x, y, and z, and by using these you can define any location, or point, in space.

# 3D modeling

Everything else in 3D modeling is built on this basis. Connect three points to form a triangle, and you have a polygon, or face. Join a number of faces together, and you can create any object. In practice, you no longer have to build objects point by point or face by face, as there are sophisticated tools that let you work much more efficiently.

The face, or "poly," is one type of geometry in 3D, but there are others. Curves can be created, as in 2D drawing programs, and used as the starting point for more complex objects. To create a pipe in the shape of an S, for example, first draw

a path by placing points in the familiar way. Then draw the cross-section, in this case a simple circle. Finally, extend the profile along the path to create a 3D pipe. This process is called sweeping. The surface created might be polygonal, or (depending on the 3D software you are using) formed from Béziers or Non Uniform Rational B-Splines (NURBS).

Béziers and NURBS are special types of geometry whose surface is defined by mathematical equations. The former are familiar from 2D illustration software. Objects created using

Left: Subdivision surfaces combine polygons with independent surfaces of NURBS-like resolution and are ideal for creating organic forms. The outer "cage," which has few points and faces, controls the inner smooth surface beneath. Because there are fewer points on the cage, it is easy to edit to change the shape of the surface beneath.

3D ILLUSTRATION

these geometries still have points, but unlike polygon objects they do not have faces. Surfaces are therefore continuous rather than faceted, making them particularly useful for organic objects, where tight curves need to remain smooth and flowing. When it comes to rendering a surface, however, the 3D software must freeze the object into a polygon mesh so that it can be shaded. The benefit is that the density of the mesh generated—that is, the number of polygons required to construct it—can be precisely controlled, so that at any distance from the object it appears smooth, unlike a conventional polygonal model. NURBS and Béziers are therefore said to be resolution independent.

3D programs also come with a stock of primitives. These are ready-made 3D objects that you can add to your scene and assemble into more complex forms. For example, to make a table you first create five cubes. Four are stretched along the y-axis to make legs, and the fifth is stretched along the x- and z-axes to form the top.

Procedurals are a special class of primitive object. In effect, these are small programs that

Above: NURBS surfaces are well suited to organic modeling and characters. Models such as this alien head can be created by stitching together various NURBS surfaces. Unlike other kinds of 3D geometry, you can create blends and fillets between NURBS surfaces to make smooth, seamless joins.

The model (left) is displayed with an isoparm wireframe overlay, enabling you to see its structure. NURBS are resolution independent, so when rendered (right) there are no visible faceted edges, even when viewed close up, as would inevitably be the case with polygon objects.

generate 3D objects. Procedural objects often have controls that can be accessed to change parameters such as radius, the rounding of edges, or polygonal resolution.

A final common geometry type is the subdivision surface. This combines the hands-on nature of polygons with the resolution independence of NURBS. You can use most of the standard polygon tools, but do not have to worry about your objects appearing faceted. Subdivision surfaces can be used to create any kind of object, but they tend to be suited to organic objects such as characters.

LIGHTING in 3D is just like lighting for film or photography—more or less. However, a computer enables you to manipulate any form of light, such as sunlight, in any way you choose. As in real life, an unlit scene would be invisible when rendered. Within your scene, you can place four main types of light: spotlights, point lights, distant (or parallel) lights, and ambient light.

# Lighting

**4**

To cast a cone of light onto a subject, as on a stage, you use a spotlight. Spotlights are very practical, since their illumination can be focused on one particular area. Point lights are good for simulating a lightbulb, camp-fire, or any other type of light that is cast from one location and dispersed in every direction.

For an exterior, however, you may want the effect of natural sunlight, and for this a distant light is most suitable, because it acts like a light source infinitely far away from the subject. Ambient light does not have a location or direction, but illuminates all parts of a 3D scene equally. You would use ambient light to decrease the contrast of hard black shadow areas in a scene, for example. Many 3D artists prefer not to use it, and instead fake ambient lighting using one or more of the other light types.

There is another form of light called an area light. This is similar to a point light, except that its source of illumination is spread over an area, normally a square or disc. You can use area lights to simulate a photographer's light diffuser, or an open window.

Aside from the way they illuminate objects, the various types of light also cast shadows in their own specific ways. Distant lights and spotlights will cast very different-looking shadows, because their rays travel in different ways (radi-

**Studio lighting setup**
Opposite top: A simple three-point lighting setup is easy to achieve, and mimics similar setups used in photography. Our scene is a simple 3D character that needs to be clearly lit. Begin by adding a single spot (shown as a white cone in the wireframe), which is the key light. Notice that much of one side of the object is still in darkness.

Opposite center: A fill light is added (shown as a black cone here) to fill in the area in shadow. Importantly, it is not as bright as the key light, but

about 40% of its brightness. The fill is positioned on the opposite side of the camera to the key. There's still a problem: the black body does not stand out from the background.

Opposite bottom: To fix this, the third light comes into play. Two bright kicker lights—also known as backlights or rim lights—are added behind the object (marked in white, left and bottom) and positioned so that, from the camera view (marked in green), they catch highlights on the character, making it pop out from the dark background.

ally in the case of a point light; in parallel in the case of a distant light). These two light types also use a process called raytracing (see page 152) to enable their shadows to take into account the transparency of surfaces. Raytraced shadows are usually hard-edged, and can look unrealistic. Soft-edged raytraced shadows, such as those cast by area lights, can be rendered, but are

# Lighting

computationally expensive, which in practical terms means rendering can take a very long time.

Spotlights can raytrace, too, but they can also use depth maps. These render quickly, as long as sufficient memory is available in the computer. Depth map shadows' edges can be variably blurred to create realistic soft shadows—not as realistic as area shadows, but usually convincing. On the other hand, depth map shadows do not usually take into account surface transparency, although Cinema 4D XL can pull this off.

A good place to start when lighting in 3D is to use the traditional photographer's two-point light setup. A spotlight is used as the main light, or key, while a second, dimmer spot or point light fills in the shadows. This is called the fill, and is usually placed on the opposite side from the key light. So if the key light is above and to the right, the fill will be on the left, level with the object or slightly below. The fill is often moved backward away from the key.

A three-point lighting rig adds a third back-light, sometimes called a rim or kicker light. This is positioned behind the object and either above, below, or to the side, so that it just catches its edge. Rim lighting is useful for pulling an object out against a dark background.

Left: Using raytraced (hard) shadows, you can take advantage of the ability to create effects such as this transparent colored shadow. This simple example is not intended to look realistic—the shadow is too sharp—but demonstrates a useful trick for generating patterns of light for illustration purposes.

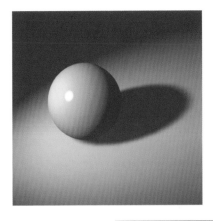

Although your basic lighting setup may resemble a real-world rig, it would be unusual to rely entirely on a simulation of physical lighting to render a scene. A useful trick of virtual lighting is that lights can be set to a negative value. This removes illumination from a scene wherever they "shine." Negative lights are good for mopping up light spillage and for darkening areas of a scene that look over-illuminated.

Left: Ambient light illuminates all parts of a scene evenly, having neither location nor direction. It tends to lighten the shadow areas of a scene, reducing overall contrast. Here, 30% ambient illumination is used with a normal spotlight.

Right: The main types of light (clockwise from left) are spot, point, distant, and area. Notice the difference in illumination on the floor plane, and both the shape and edge quality of the shadow cast. In each case, the exact lighting qualities are a direct result of the light's properties: location, direction, and size.

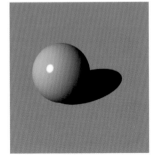

**TEXTURING** Applying textures is a vital technique for making models appear more natural, and more like the objects they are intended to represent. For newcomers, it is also one of the more confusing aspects of 3D illustration.

# Texturing

3D programs enable you to use a bitmap—whether a photo or an image painted from scratch—to create surface detail on objects. The bitmap is wrapped around the object using a projection. This can be thought of as curving the flat image in space, enveloping the object, then shining light inward through it onto the object's surface. Where light strikes the object, the texture will appear. This is called projection mapping, or just mapping, and can be used with movie files or sequences as well as still images.

The shape of the projection can vary. For example, to map a flat plane you can use a planar projection parallel to the object surface. To map a sphere, a spherical projection is used. The shape of the projection, however, is independent of the shape of the object.

The obvious use for a texture map is to provide color and pattern, but maps can also control

Right: Mapping textures to objects involves using projections. Here are some standard projections used in 3D, applied to objects of similar shape. Left to right—spherical, cubic, cylindrical, and planar. In practice, of course, you will rarely be mapping such simple objects.

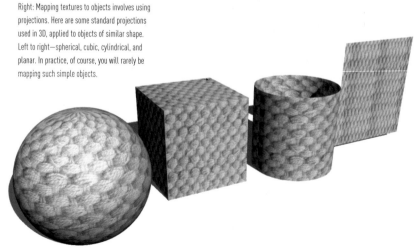

other properties of the surface, such as its shininess, transparency, or bumpiness. Here, the texture is created in grayscale—whiter parts let the surface's original property show through, while blacker parts mask it out. For example, to add a label to a bottle, you first create an image map of a black square on a white background, and apply it using a cylindrical projection to the transparency property of the bottle. Where the texture map is white, the glass will be transparent, where it is black, it will be opaque, forming the label. A separate RGB image could then be applied to the label to add its printed message.

To help keep these maps together, 3D programs use the concept of a material, which contains all the surface property settings and maps for a particular kind of surface. The material is usually independent from the object it is applied to as well as the projection used, so it can easily be applied to any object in your scene.

When creating a 3D object, the trick is to know where to stop modeling and begin texturing. It is surprising how little detail is often needed in the geometry, and how much can be supplied by textures.

Bump maps are used to take over where geometry leaves off. A bump map is a grayscale image map whose brightness values create virtual perturbations on the surfaces of an object. (A similar effect can be used in 2D software—see page 56.) White in the map causes a bump, black a dip. These surface bumps only change the shading of the object; they do not change its geometry, so lights will not create additional highlights on their peaks or shadows in their troughs. But the details in a bump map can be infinitely finer than the geometry of the model. The only limit is how big the map resolution is and how close the camera can get to the surface.

A typical use of a bump map is the rendering of human skin. There is no need to model each

Right: Choosing the right projection for an object is usually a compromise. To illustrate, a sphere has been mapped using each of the four projections. Some look a lot better than others—notice how the planar texture is smearing around the edges of the sphere.

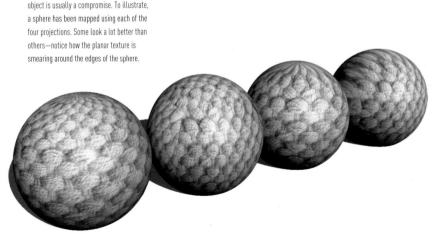

# Texturing

### Modeling with displacement maps

Right: It is possible to create an entire model by displacement, and thus avoid time-consuming geometry. Here is an image we want to turn into a 3D model. The background is 50% gray, indicating no displacement. The image is white, so it will rise above the surface, and is slightly blurred to round the edges.

Right: In the 3D program (Maya in this case), a NURBS plane is created. A material is assigned to the object and the image is loaded, and applied as a displacement map. Test rendering shows the displacement is occurring, but the resolution of the NURBS object is insufficient to create the fine detail required.

tiny fold, crease, or pore, because all this detail can be created using bump maps.

Displacement maps are similar to bump maps, but they move the geometry to which they are applied. As such, displacements depend on the geometry of the object being fine enough to recreate the detail in the map. While this is tricky for polygon models, it is ideal for NURBS, since the surface can be created during rendering with any resolution you like. A clever technique is to use animations or movie files as displacement maps to create effects such as undulating water.

Left: The tessellation on the NURBS surface is increased, so that it is subdivided many times into tiny triangles before the surface is displaced. The result is that the bitmap is accurately represented in the displaced geometry. Note that, because it is a real displacement of the geometry, it casts shadows.

Left: In Maya, you can go one step further and convert what will be rendered into a polygonal object. The displacement is now seen as geometry, and you can continue to model the resulting object as normal. In this way you could build up a finished, realistic object without ever doing any modeling as such.

RENDERING is the process of creating a 2D image or animation from the 3D data you have created. Whether it is a simple sphere or an entire city, a human character, or an assemblage of abstract forms makes no difference. The software uses a process called shading to fill in the surfaces with color, taking into account the scene lighting and textures you have applied.

# Rendering

To do this, the software must have a point of view from which to render. This is provided by a camera, which you place within your scene, adjusting its field of view (zoom) as required. The camera is also used to view the 3D scene during modeling and setup. There are other kinds of views as well, notably the three orthographic or parallel views that look down the three world axes. You can place multiple cameras and switch between them. When rendering, cameras, and characters, can be moved through time to build up a movie.

Because high-quality rendering takes time, various display options are used. Display rendering is usually accelerated using OpenGL, a standardized set of graphics commands for both 3D software and graphics cards, enabling the latter to process the display very efficiently. Objects can be viewed fully shaded, with textures and lighting taken into account. Even effects such as reflections, fog, depth of field, and motion blur can be displayed very quickly. However, OpenGL is not a final-quality rendering process.

If all other aspects, such as texturing, have been correctly set up, the final image quality depends on the rendering. If you render the scene pixel-for-pixel at the size required, you will get aliasing, or jagged edges. To smooth this out, the software uses anti-aliasing, which adds to the rendering time but produces far superior images.

Most 3D programs offer adaptive anti-aliasing, which smooths only pixels that need it, based on a threshold set by you, and speeds up rendering. Some programs, such as 3ds Max and Cinema 4D XL, offer a choice of anti-aliasing algorithms.

Raytracing is a technique that can be combined with shading to create effects such as reflections, refractions and transparent shadows. It shines imaginary light rays onto the scene, tracing their paths as they strike objects.

Thanks to advances in software and computer power, there are now more techniques that take into account lighting effects—specifically, the way light is bounced between objects. Global illumination and radiosity rendering produce very realistic images with a natural warmth and ambience.

Global illumination lets you do away with scene lighting altogether and use an image to light your scene. A special HDRI (high dynamic range imagery) bitmap encircles the scene, and its brighter portions act like light sources, casting its illumination and color onto objects, so you can recreate with breathtaking realism the lighting of any real location. Creating HDRI images is quite an involved process, but ready-made examples are freely available online. LightWave 3D is currently the only 3D application that directly supports HDRI rendering, while most others offer radiosity and global illumination.

Left: HDRI images store floating-point brightness values that can be much greater than traditional 24-bit color files. When such an image is used in a 3D program as a source of illumination with radiosity rendering, the results are highly realistic, since the scene lighting mimics the lighting at the time the HDRI image was captured. A "light probe" image of a forest (inset) has been used in LightWave 3D as a spherical environment background for the rendering of the teapot.

Right: Depth of field (DOF) rendering simulates the shallow depth of field obtainable with real large-aperture lens and camera systems. Some portions of the image are blurred and others in focus, depending on the object's distance. You have complete control over the degree of the effect, and results can be very photographic.

Left: Raytracing takes longer than normal shading methods, but can simulate natural effects such as reflection and refraction. By plotting the paths of millions of light rays through the scene, a renderer can precisely recreate these phenomena, which would otherwise be impossible to represent accurately.

**COMBINING A 2D** image-editing program such as Adobe Photoshop with a 3D package enables you to get the best of both worlds. Individual renders can be brought into Photoshop for final tweaks to overall levels and color balance in the scene, or to smooth over minor rendering glitches. Or, having rendered a number of 3D objects separately, you might composite them all into an illustration.

# 3D into 2D

It is important to plan this type of work before you render, and make sure you render out an alpha channel so that each 3D element can be separated from its background. Most 3D programs can save into bitmap formats, such as TIFF, with an embedded alpha channel. Or, the alpha can be saved in a separate file and re-applied in Photoshop.

If there is more than one object in the scene, the 3D software will need to know what to include in the alpha channel. For example, if you rendered a sphere resting on an infinite floor plane, viewed from above, you might expect the alpha channel to show a disc surrounding the sphere, but in fact it would be completely white. An obvious solution would be to delete the floor before rendering. However, in many cases you may want to include background objects in a rendering, though not in

the alpha channel, and it would be needlessly time consuming to render each on its own. To get around this, many 3D programs let you set whether each object will appear in the alpha channel. Making full use of workflow enhancements like this is essential to advanced 3D work, since render time is such a large part of your efficiency.

It is quicker to change something in 2D than in 3D. If the client decides the color of a logo in a scene needs changing from blue to red, you could make the alteration in 3D and re-render. But it is far quicker to do it in Photoshop using the previously rendered image. Of course, if the client wanted a sequence of illustrations showing the scene from different angles, and you had not yet rendered the others, it might be quicker to make the change in 3D than to re-color all the logos in

Left: This 3D object has been rendered and saved as a TIFF. We now have two layers, each with a mask created from the relevant alpha channel generated by the 3D program. The star's mask matches its alpha channel, so anything outside itself will show. The circle has the reverse alpha channel, so only parts that do not overlap the star are seen.

Inset: A masked element placed over a color different to the background on which it was rendered will have a dark or light halo around it. The anti-aliasing applied to the edge of the object during rendering combines the colors of the object and background pixels. To avoid this, simply set the background to the same color in your 3D program.

4

Left and below left: When compositing volumetric effects, such as light shining through dust or smoke, a good choice is the Straight Alpha option. Rather than applying these effects to the background itself during rendering, the software then places only the transparency information, which creates the effect, in the alpha channel. When compositing in Photoshop, you can use this to apply the volumetric effect over any background.

Photoshop. More often, though, changing something after rendering will be quicker. Many 3D programs now make post-processing of renderings even easier by offering multipass rendering.

With multipass rendering, the different components of an image are saved as individual files, or as layers within a Photoshop PSD file. What we mean by components is not separate objects, but different material and illumination information. So highlights alone will be on one layer, color on another, diffuse shading on a third, shadows on yet another, and so on. The great plus is that it does not take significantly longer, since internally

the 3D software calculates all these "buffers" separately anyway.

Armed with a multilayered rendering, you can select just the highlights in Photoshop and use Levels to brighten them, or duplicate the layer and blur it for specular blooming effects. You have similar control over any other property, including reflections, luminance, and sometimes even radiosity. In Cinema 4D XL you can also save out each light's diffuse, specular, and shadow contributions as separate layers (arranged in layer folders in the PSD file), enabling you to adjust lighting even after the final rendering.

# ANIMATION

# 5

# DIGITAL ANIMATION

**5**

**WHERE ANIMATION** has traditionally been a painfully slow process—moving each element frame by frame a tiny amount—the digital solution removes much of the drudgery, and lets the animator concentrate on the more creative aspects.

Although the process of frame-by-frame motion is largely automated by software, digital animation still requires painstaking attention to detail. The software can do the more repetitive tasks, but the artist needs to keep track of the dozens of individual objects or layers that make up a scene.

All animation programs use a timeline system—a chart showing individual frames or timings (in seconds) along the horizontal axis, with a list of the animation elements on the vertical axis. Often, a component will have several attributes such as size, rotation, and color, which can be set individually.

Elements of the animation—whether 3D objects, photomontages, or drawn images—are positioned at user-specified keyframes on the timeline. The programs use a system called "tweening" to generate the object positions for every frame between two keyframes: if a figure has its arm by its side in frame one, and raised above its head in frame 30, the computer works out the arm position for each intermediate frame. Effects, such as motion blur, give a better impression of movement by preventing the motion from looking stilted.

Animations for movies and TV are usually generated at 24 or 25 frames per second, but websites usually use a far lower frame rate—each frame in an animation is a separate image, and for Internet delivery the higher rate would result in files too large to be downloaded smoothly. Since most website animations use a "streaming" process, where movies begin playing before they have completely downloaded, it is important to ensure that the download is always ahead of the play position of the movie to avoid stops and starts.

Although you need to specify a frame rate for an animation, you do not have to stick to it for the output. A test render of a movie at half the normal frame rate, or less, will result in a far quicker rendering that will still show how the animation works—even if it is a little jerky in this preview state.

Opposite: Kaya is an award-winning project by Alceu Baptistão, a founding director of production company Vetor Zero, to create an animated human face that appears natural and "alive." Rather than dedicated facial modeling tools, the standard functions of Maya were used in conjunction with textures painted in Adobe Photoshop.
ALCEU BAPTISTÃO
WWW.VETORZERO.COM/KAYA

**ADOBE FLASH** is the main choice for illustrators looking to create a range of animated content. The popularity of the Flash format and the widespread availability of its browser plug-ins have made Flash animation a standard feature on ambitious websites. The package itself is actually three applications in one: an animation tool and sequencer; an interactive multimedia authoring environment; and a vector-drawing program.

# Flash

Thanks to these hybrid features, it is capable of creating a broad range of animated and/or interactive content, from website intros, banner adverts, and navigation bars to broadcast-quality cartoons. Added to this, Flash includes its own highly robust programming language, ActionScript based on JavaScript, which has become one of the world's most popular programming languages. ActionScript enables Flash content to work with other web-based systems and resources, such as databases, so it can be integrated with the most advanced delivery systems.

We are mainly concerned here with the vector animation capabilities of Flash, which are both powerful and suitable for many types of work. Although Flash is capable of animating bitmaps and even handling full-motion video content, its native file format is vector-based, and this is where its core strengths lie. Unlike Adobe Director, Flash relies on its low-bandwidth vector format to transmit the animation via the web. Most Internet users will have encountered Flash content on hundreds of websites, whether as overt graphical content or in enhanced navigation features.

Above: Flash, like other animation tools, offers "onion skinning" as an aid to the animation process. The current frame's artwork is overlaid semi-transparently with the illustrations in the prior and subsequent frames, so you can make adjustments taking these into account.

Flash movies are very compact, and download fairly rapidly even on modem-based connections. However, standard web browsers, such as Microsoft Internet Explorer and Safari, need a Flash Player plug-in before they can display Flash content. Although over 20 million users have already installed this free download, most site owners still recognize the need to provide

ANIMATION

parallel, non-Flash content to ensure material is universally accessible.

Flash provides a wide variety of vector drawing tools with which to create characters and backgrounds, and you can also add imported vector graphics, bitmaps, or video clips to your movies. For video playback, Flash uses Sorenson Spark encoding and playback technology, which enables very high quality video to be streamed at low connection speeds over the Internet.

Central to Flash is a powerful animation sequencer. The organization of sequences, or movies, is achieved using a variety of methods. Each Flash movie can contain any number of scenes, which can be arranged in any playing order. ActionScript commands can be applied to individual objects within a scene or to the whole scene. Each scene can contain an unlimited number of layers, which are viewed from front to back in the scene, as in an ordinary vector drawing. The stacking order of layers is arranged inside a familiar timeline: the top layer in the timeline appears at the front of the scene, and the bottom layer at the back. There is also a stacking order within each layer, and at the top of this—called the overlay level—are special types of object, such as bitmaps, text, grouped items, and symbol instances. Symbol instances, as in vector drawing programs, are references to an object stored once for all in a Flash library file.

A series of frames within a sequence of scenes is thus built up to make a movie. Within each frame of the movie you can have elements that change size, position, and color from the previous frame. Using scenes, you can organize sequences of frames within a movie, and link multiple scenes and movies together to complete a longer animation. You can also create traditional frame-by-frame animation using a separate image for each frame, and tweening is offered to automate the creation of intermediate frames between start and end images.

Above: Once you have built all the separate animated elements for your scene, the best way to build an animation is to convert each element into an animated symbol. Symbols can be animated, static, or interactive.

Here, we have converted our animated objects into Flash symbols, and we are now ready to start building a complete animated scene. (Bottom) Flash creates the inbetween frames in a sequence through "tweening."

Right: Flash has some useful features that let you organize a scene to make it easier and more productive to animate. Once all your symbols have been created, the next step is to create a series of hierarchical layers in the timeline, where they can reside. Here, we have set all the elements in their

own layers and positioned them for the first keyframe of the scene.

**ADOBE AFTER EFFECTS** is a powerful animation program that combines still images with movies and sound. Designed to work with Photoshop, it can open files from that application directly—each layer in Photoshop will be retained as a separate object in After Effects. This means that it is possible to build an entire animation, element by element, in Photoshop; opening the file in After Effects lets all the elements be animated.

# After Effects

**5**

The range of animation techniques employed by the program is extensive. Simple effects include rotation, scaling, and movement of objects over time—the most basic animation controls. Motion events can be triggered automatically by movies or sound files; the size of a split in a figure's mouth can be determined by the volume of an audio file, making the figure's lips move in time with recorded speech to give a reasonable impression of talking.

More sophisticated effects are also available, such as the ability to vary the color, opacity, and

sharpening of a layer. Several Photoshop plug-in filters, such as Ripple, Spherize, and Lens Flare, can also be animated over time. In addition, After Effects includes a unique 3D engine, whereby flat images are arranged in a virtual 3D space; they can then be rotated and viewed from any angle, made to cast shadows, and so on.

Motion in After Effects is controlled by a timeline. Colored bars show the length of time for which an object is visible, while controls for each object indicate the angle of rotation, scaling, or

ANIMATION

**head/KEN** used 1 time
265 x 401, D1/DV PAL (1.07)

Millions of Colors+ (Straight)

| Name | 🖳 | Type | Size | Durat |
|------|-----|------|------|-------|
| ▽ 📁 KEN | | 🔲 Folder | | |
| 🐾 body/KEN | | 🔲 Photoshop | 4.4M | |
| 🐾 eye/KEN | | 🔲 Photoshop | 4.4M | |
| 🐾 eyeball/KEN | | 🔲 Photoshop | 4.4M | |
| 🐾 eyelids/KEN | | 🔲 Photoshop | 4.4M | |
| 🐾 fist/KEN | | 🔲 Photoshop | 4.4M | |
| 🐾 handL/KEN | | 🔲 Photoshop | 4.4M | |
| 🐾 handR/KEN | | 🔲 Photoshop | 4.4M | |
| 🐾 head/KEN | | 🔲 Photoshop | 4.4M | |
| 🐾 Layer 2/KEN | | 🔲 Photoshop | 4.4M | |
| 🐾 Layer 3/KEN | | 🔲 Photoshop | 4.4M | |
| 🐾 moutha/KEN | | 🔲 Photoshop | 4.4M | |
| 🐾 moutho/KEN | | 🔲 Photoshop | 4.4M | |

Above: All the images and sounds used in a project are referenced through a single palette. This indicates the size, type, and location of the original files, and lets each be previewed in isolation.

degree of special effect at each point. Tweening, where intermediary steps are calculated between keyframes, applies to all the parameters of a chosen object, so a Lens Flare filter, for example, may be set to gradually build to full strength by setting the opacity at 0% and 100% at two keyframes. By adding a third keyframe marking its focal point in a different position, an object can be made to move across the image area. Drawing a curved path between the second and third keyframes will make the flare follow that path rather than a straight line. The result will be a spotlight fading into view and then panning smoothly across the scene.

After Effects is designed for creating animations for TV and movie display, as well as for multimedia and web projects. Since it uses high-resolution still images, there need be no concerns about the broadcast quality of footage. Many professional television title sequences are created using After Effects, as the results can be output to a range of standard movie formats.

Far left: The animation is previewed in its own window, which may be set to a variety of sizes. The rectangles inside the image area show the Action Safe and Title Safe areas for film and TV use.

Left: The timeline shows the length of each picture and sound element; for each image the length of its "bat" indicates the time in which it will be visible in the finished animation.

**TOON BOOM STUDIO** is a complete 2D animation application that is ideal for web graphics and multimedia applications. Novice digital illustrators may find that it suits their needs better than Adobe Flash. While most new media animators have settled on Adobe Director or Flash, neither is very attractive to traditional animators who want to work in a digital environment. Toon Boom Studio is aimed at the professional animator who needs a tool for the sole purpose of emulating traditional animation techniques.

# Toon Boom Studio

Based on US Animation, Toon Boom Studio uses Flash graphics and animation technology, omitting the interactive capabilities. The entire program is based on tried and tested animation production techniques, and as a result it is exceptionally efficient. Work of an impressive quality can be created with relative ease, and even newcomers to the field may find Toon Boom suits their purposes better than Flash.

Toon Boom Studio has two modes of working: Drawing and Scene Planning. All the graphic ele-

ments of an animation are created, manipulated, and inked in Drawing mode. Scene Planning brings these elements into a scene layout window and timeline, where you can manipulate the position and behavior of every object, in space and time.

The Drawing mode offers graphic tools that are similar to those in Flash but arguably easier to handle. The brush tools, for instance, are pressure sensitive, which makes it easy for users with conventional drawing skills and a graphics tablet to create expressive illustrations that

Left: Toon Boom Studio offers two interfaces—one for drawing and one for scene planning. Here in Drawing mode, you have access to a traditional animator's field chart and a series of basic vector drawing tools. The exposure sheet is similar to a traditional animator's column-based spreadsheet for the management of each frame and cel.

resemble traditional inked cels. Ink fills can be applied separately using a Paint tool, and you can use Custom Shapes to close any open paths you have created. Text is not supported, but it can be imported from another drawing program via the most popular vector formats.

In the Scene Planning mode, you can arrange your drawings using a form of 3D object positioning based on three different planes: background, midfield, and foreground. Elements are arranged in view of the virtual camera, with scenery at the back, and actors and other objects stacked toward the front. You can adjust distances using Top and Side Views as well as Object Properties. When your animation is rendered, objects become larger and smaller according to their distance from the camera, and this perspective is maintained as both objects and the camera are moved and manipulated. The results are really quite sophisticated, and would be tricky and time consuming to produce if you were manually scaling 2D artwork in a single plane.

There are two methods of animating your illustrations. The first is to assign one or more objects to "pegs" that you can then "tween" inside the Scene Planning timeline, with the motion of the various pegged objects governed by Bézier-style control paths. The second method uses the concept of an exposure sheet, accessed in Drawing mode. Here you can create very complex animations using a single graphic element with multiple layers, each of which is separately animated. Such objects can be incorporated into a larger scene by linking them into the timeline as they play through their own frames.

Toon Boom's Lip Synchronization feature is unique among vector programs, and makes it far easier to create cartoon characters that talk. The software analyzes imported sound clips, automatically adding example graphics, key points, and labels into the audio track. From there, it is easy to arrange illustrated facial graphics inside the exposure sheet to match, and tie down audio highlights to the visual highlights you have drawn.

Left: The Scene Planning mode is the heart of Toon Boom Studio. You have access to several views including a camera view, a horizontal timeline, and top and side diagrammatic camera views. Control is provided over the tracking of a camera throughout a scene. With the top and side viewing planes, you can move the camera, using complex trajectories, through a flexible and automated multiplane system.

**ANIMATED GIFS** One of the features that differentiates web pages from printed material is the use of animation. Flash and QuickTime movies are one option, but they rely on the user having downloaded the appropriate plug-ins in order to view them. They can also be very memory intensive.

# Animated GIFs

Animated GIFs are a simple, easy-to-make alternative. They load just like regular graphics, and can be "optimized" to make them as small as possible. This process is a trade-off between image quality and file size—generally speaking, the lower the quality, the smaller the file.

Image quality depends on several factors: the number of colors used; the "dithering" method (a way of simulating missing colors by placing similar shades in close proximity); and the overall "lossiness" of the image. The greater the difference between each frame and the previous one, the

Below: This mock-up of a holiday advertisement uses several animation techniques. The plane approaches us through the clouds, and flies overhead. This is accomplished by using three different plane layers at different sizes, with only one visible at a time. The first six frames use the same-sized plane, which is moved a little at each frame to simulate

motion. The word "Worldwide" has a layer mask, which gradually slides to the right, frame by frame, to reveal the whole word; the word "holidays" is faded in gradually over three frames until it reaches 100% opacity. The sunburst is created as three separate applications of the Lens Flare filter, increasing the strength of the filter each time.

larger the file size will be. Often, only a tiny change can be enough to gain a sense of movement.

Animated GIF files have the additional advantage that they can be viewed from any web browser, without any special software or plug-ins being required. They are normally small page elements, and are generally set to repeat or "loop" the animation they contain. Banner advertising on websites usually comprises a single GIF file that repeats endlessly. With many websites insisting that advertisements must be no more than 10K in size, it is down to the skill of the animator to produce the best-looking advertisement in the smallest file size.

There are many programs for creating animated GIFs. One of the most popular, Adobe ImageReady, is now built into Adobe Photoshop as the Animation panel. Animations are typically created on a frame-by-frame basis using Photoshop layers. Image elements can be moved between frames, and their position logged for that frame only. Other transformations, such as scaling and rotation, apply globally, so in the

Worldwide Holidays mock-up shown here, three different versions of the plane are required since it appears at three sizes.

The visibility of objects can be controlled on a frame-by-frame basis, and you can preview the animation directly in Photoshop using the playback controls in the Animation panel. Finally, you can experiment with different output settings to optimize the final product for appearance and file size. This is far from the only way to create animated GIFs, but it is certainly among the most flexible and powerful ways to work.

However, don't expect too much from this format; full photographic color isn't strictly possible, and long animation sequences can lead to large files no matter how you tweak the settings.

**3D ANIMATION** offers the most creative opportunities of any digital medium, but it also imposes one of the steepest learning curves. Various special techniques are used to help you control the way animation occurs over time.

# 3D Animation

3D works pretty much like animation in other kinds of programs, in that you start with a timeline and keyframes, which are interpolated over time to create motion. What makes it a lot more complex is that there are three spatial dimensions in which objects, cameras, and lights can all move and rotate.

To help control the way animation occurs over time, 3D programs often use function curves. In the case of the movement, or translation, of an object in space, these curves control the x, y, and z directions. For example, if an object is set at x = 10 at frame one, and x = 30 at frame 50, its motion will be described by the shape of a function curve between these two keyframes.

If the motion is linear—that is, the object moves at a constant rate and does not speed up or slow down as it travels—the function curve will be a straight line. To create an "ease in, ease out" animation, where the object accelerates smoothly from a standing start, travels linearly, and then decelerates to a standstill again, you would manipulate the function curve into an S shape. Function curves are usually controlled via Bézier handles, although many 3D programs also let you use other kinds of keyframe interpolation, such as stepped, linear, cubic, and TCB (tension, continuity, and bias).

Animation in 3D is heavily dependent on hierarchies. A hierarchy is a grouping of objects that provides a child–parent relationship between the occupants of the group. If you move or animate a parent, its children will move along with it. Hierarchies also let you build complex jointed objects whose limbs can easily be animated.

Traditional animation uses a process called forward kinematics, or FK. To animate a leg taking a step, you keyframe the hip, then the thigh, then the shin, then the foot, at each section of the animation, one by one until the step is mapped out. It works, but is cumbersome.

Now, though, 3D programs enable you to animate using inverse kinematics, or IK. To take a step using IK, you just move the foot—the shin, thigh, and hip then move right along with it. Or, rather, they rotate. The beauty of IK is that the hierarchy does not fall apart when you pull on one end of it. An IK'ed leg requires keyframes only for the foot; the rotations of the other joints are calculated on a frame by frame basis by the software.

Using IK is all very well for a jointed hierarchy, but how do you go about animating a character, for example, that is made of a single mesh without jointed sections? In this case, you build a hierarchy out of special non-rendering objects known as bones (or sometimes joints). The bones form a skeleton inside the single-skinned

Above: Function curves display the interpolation between keyframes as a curve in a graph. The shape of the curve helps you visualize the way the object moves between keyframes. A straight curve means there is no acceleration or deceleration.

Left: A typical function curve shape is an S. This gives an object a smooth motion that starts and stops naturally, without any jerkiness. The way you shape your curves can greatly influence the dynamic feel of your animations.

# 3D Animation

character, and the skin is bound to the bones so that, as they rotate, the skin surrounding them deforms at the joints. FK and IK are then used as normal to animate the skeleton, which in turn deforms the mesh to produce the rendered animated character.

Not only objects can be animated. The camera and lights can be animated, too, and to help with the process you will often find special objects, called nulls, in use. A null is another kind of non-rendering object, and is really just a location in space defined by a set of axes and usually displayed as a cross. Objects can be parented to nulls, which are then animated. This eases the complications that arise from rotating axes in three dimensions.

Gimbal lock is one common problem, often associated with the camera, which can be solved with nulls. Here, one axis becomes rotated so that the other two axes are in the same plane; rotating either one then causes exactly the same rotation, whether you want it or not. By linking a camera to two or three nulls in a cascading hierarchy, gimbal lock is avoided. Null one is animated around the x-axis only, null two around the y-axis only, and the camera is free to be rotated in around the z-axis. If this all sounds a little tricky, that is because it is: 3D animation offers some incredible creative opportunities, but is the most demanding of all digitial media when it comes to grasping more than the basic concepts.

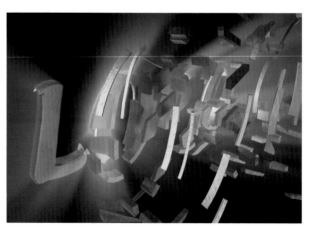

Left and opposite:
3D software lets you build all sorts of complex animations from simple components. For example, a basic logo animation can be enhanced by applying a special deformer that explodes the mesh. The parameters of the explosion can then be animated to reassemble the logo over time.

Outliner

Display   Show   Help

nurbsSphere1
  └ pCube1
      └ pCbue2
          └ pCube3
              └ pCube4

Left: Hierarchies enable you to make complex animations without trying to keep impossible numbers of objects in sync. By grouping objects in hierarchies, you can create jointed structures such as a mechanical arm. Each object rotates where it is joined to its parent, so the whole group can be manipulated together.

# ARTIST AT WORK

# THE WORKING ILLUSTRATOR

**PROFESSIONAL PRACTICE** A well-designed online portfolio is one of the primary considerations for the professional illustrator. The website itself is a representation of the illustrator's style and quality of work, as well as the images on showcase in the portfolio.

Traditionally, artists had to compile portfolios containing the best samples of their work. Keeping these portfolios up to date with the latest clippings was one problem; getting them to clients—which often meant ordering couriers or transporting them personally—could be both time consuming and costly.

Today, a digital artist can display their work on an individual website, which has the advantages of being instantly available to multiple recipients, and of being easy to update as the need arises. Web design programs are becoming much easier to use, and even with no technical expertise, it is possible for the novice to put together a convincing site.

In order to create your own website, you need two things: a domain name, and the web space itself. Buying a domain with your own name is easy if you are called, say, Vladimir Borowyczyk, since the chances of www.vladimirborowyczyk.com being taken are fairly slim. But if you are John Smith, you will need to take a different approach. Either way, the name needs to be obvious and memorable; the default names that come supplied with some web-hosting and email packages, usually along the lines of www.jsmith24.cutpricewebspace.net, are not likely to portray the professional image you would wish for.

Domain names at the "top level"—those ending in .com—cost $10 or so for every year of registration, and country-specific names cost slightly less. The cost of web space itself varies from free to around $40 (£25) a year for basic hosting. If you take the free option, be aware that your site will probably be swamped with ugly banner advertising. You can pay much more than $40 to have your web traffic monitored and statistically evaluated, but these additional services will be of little use to the typical illustrator.

Opposite: Derek Lea's high-tech work is displayed within a suitably modern environment. The thumbnails show details from the illustrations they lead to, rather than reduced versions of the whole.

Another method of distributing your work is on CD. You will need to compile some sort of front-end application to let users browse the work easily. There are many multimedia applications that will enable this, but you have to be certain of cross-platform compatibility (in other words, that the application will work on both Macs and PCs). Building a website solely for CD distribution is often a better option. With the blank media costing just a few cents, you can send CDs out to prospective clients and not worry about getting them back.

But without doubt, the best way of getting your name in front of prospective clients is for them to see your byline in a reputable publication—which means convincing an art editor to take a chance on your work. As ever, the first rung of the ladder is the hardest to reach.

**RAW TALENT** and advanced technical skills are not enough to guarantee a steady stream of work for the digital illustrator. No matter how good you are, it is vital that you adhere to a few simple rules if you want repeat work from a client.

# Working with clients

Before any art editor is prepared to commit to a new or untried illustrator, he or she needs to be satisfied that certain conditions can be met. The chief criteria are:

1. Is the style original?
2. Is the work of a sufficient standard for publication?
3. Can the illustrator interpret a brief?
4. Will the illustrator be sure to meet the deadline?

It is perhaps a sad fact that the above points have been listed in reverse order of importance. No matter how inspired or talented you may be, failing to meet the deadline will guarantee you will not be asked again. When working for magazines, artists are frequently given between two days and a week to complete an illustration. If you work for daily newspapers, the time between receiving the commission and delivering the finished artwork can be as little as a couple of hours. Miss this deadline, and the paper will be left with a blank page—which will generally be filled with a stock photograph. The cardinal rule is: do not miss deadlines.

Art editors work in a variety of ways. Some will supply you with a pencil sketch of the illustration they want, and it is up to you to make whatever changes are necessary—you are the illustrator, and you will know what works and what does not. Some art editors will simply send you the copy for the story to be illustrated, and wait for you to come up with ideas. In this case, you will either have to describe your solution over the phone (usually the way when working on tight deadlines) or supply a rough. Bear in mind, though, that if you work with photomontage, the end result will depend on what images are available, so make sure you know which elements you will want to include before drawing the rough.

Above: This is the client's original sketch for a poster for the London Zoo, to be placed on the side of a bus. The irregular shape is to fit in with the bus panels.

Interpreting a brief means finding a new, original take on a story. Avoid hackneyed or obvious solutions, and wherever possible try to avoid labeling objects within the scene. The days of a politician sitting in a boat labeled "social responsibility" tossing out a lifebelt labeled "overseas aid" are rightfully long gone.

Art editors will frequently want to make small changes to the work you supply. Keep your work in layers to maximize your ability to make adjustments, and be receptive to their suggestions—although you can argue your corner if you believe strongly that your solution is preferable. Ultimately, it is the art editor's job to get the work that he or she wants.

Advertising agencies are the most demanding of clients. Agency work will frequently go through a dozen or more alterations as everyone in the hierarchy, from the account manager to the client, pitches in with their own ideas. Ad agencies pay more than anyone else, and the sums involved can be tempting, but you will often start the job as an illustrator and end up as a mechanic, making what seem to be irrelevant and irritating changes while the art director peers over your shoulder. In cases like this, it is important that you swallow your pride and just do the job they want.

Finished artwork can be supplied by email, on CD, or via FTP for large file transfers. Work to be sent by email should be saved in highest quality JPEG format for speed of transmission, but it is not uncommon for art directors to request finished artwork in its original, layered format so that they can tweak it themselves if necessary.

Below: Because the placing of the T-section is critical, it was important to obtain precise dimensions for the shape.

Below: The original photographs of the children at the bottom were brought together to show the arrangement— but before any facial distortions were applied.

Above: The finished image with every element in place—after all of the client's amendments.

**AT SOME POINT,** you will have to discuss money with your clients. For most artists, this can be the most difficult part of the job. Pitch too high and you may price yourself out of the market; too low and your work may not be valued.

# Taking the money

Magazines and newspapers generally have standard rates for illustrations, depending on the size of the work used and the position within the publication—so an illustration for a cover, for example, will pay a premium rate. For historical reasons, publications still pay less for black-and-white (known as "mono") illustrations than for full-color work. This harks back to the days when pictures were hand drawn, and adding color was an additional process. Today, however, it is as quick to work in color as it is in mono; in fact, mono illustrations are much harder to create, as the color element—which can be used to make the focus of the image stand out—is missing. Creating an eye-catching illustration in black and white is a far more difficult process.

Advertising agencies generally have no fixed rate for illustration work. When discussing money, you will not be dealing with the art director, but with the account executive (the person responsible for the entire campaign) or, in larger agencies, the "traffic manager" (the person responsible for ensuring that everything arrives on time, in the right place). These people will have a figure in mind for the job, but they will never tell you what it is. It is up to you to come up with a price and pitch it to them. If they accept straightaway, you will know that you have pitched too low. But by that time it is too late—you cannot bargain upward. The trick is to think of the maximum amount you think the job could be worth, and then double it. Then double it again, and practice saying the amount you want in front of the mirror until you can pitch it with a straight face. When working for ad agencies, the more you charge, the more they will think you are worth.

Sending out invoices—and collecting the checks—is another important task. Invoices can be set up using a simple word processor, and printed out, but be sure to keep copies of all the invoices you send, both in order to send reminders when they become overdue (a far too common occurrence) and to keep records for tax purposes. A better solution is to use a database application to create an invoicing system, which will automatically store new invoices as separate records, and will let you sort them by date, client, paid date, and so on. There are several dedicated packages for producing invoices, but even the most basic database applications will generally suffice.

One solution to all this is to employ an agent. Agents have two main functions: to get you work, and to deal with the administrative side of the business. They get work for you by promoting you through their own websites, through mailshots and visits to advertising agencies, and by advertising in trade annuals. They will also negotiate fees and contracts, invoice clients, and chase payments. A typical fee for this service is 30% of the revenues you receive for each job they negotiate for you.

Working with an agent can be a good way for the novice illustrator to get into the business. The better agents will assess your work and may suggest ways to make it more commercially appealing, which can be a useful asset for the beginner. Some agents specialize in particular illustrative styles, while others will attempt to create a rounded portfolio consisting of a variety of styles. Before you approach an agent, check out their website to see if they seem appropriate. An Internet search for a topic such as "illustration" will turn up dozens of agency sites.

Unless you are adept at tax evasion, you will need the services of an accountant. Good accountants can save you more than they cost you, but be sure to firm up the fee situation before you commit yourself to any individual or company.

Below: Agents can find you new work, and will take care of the administrative side of the business—in return for 30% of your fees—and a good accountant will save you more than he or she costs you. At the very least, your accountant will save you the pain of filling in your own tax return.

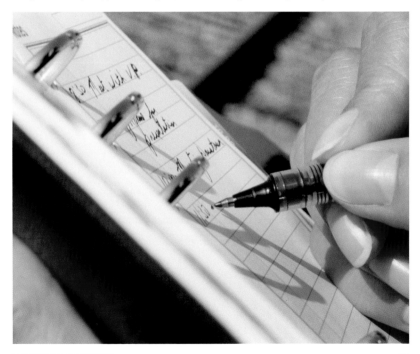

**ENSHRINED** in the intellectual property laws of most countries, copyright protects you from plagiarism and unauthorized exploitation of your work. At the same time, it limits your own use of work originated by others.

# Copyright and image sourcing

**6**

The advent of digital technology has had less impact on the fundamental principles of copyright than is popularly assumed, but the ease with which material can now be copied and published does make it more essential than ever for both illustrators and their clients to understand those principles.

In general, when you create any original artistic work you automatically become its copyright holder, and it may not be reproduced without your permission. Copyright in work produced in the course of employment, however, normally resides with your employer.

Although it is more usual for illustrators to work on a self-employed basis, the dividing line between freelance and employed work, or "work for hire," varies between countries, and it is important to be clear which side you are on.

When you sell work to a client, you are usually offering a limited license to reproduce it. A publisher would traditionally license an illustration for single use in a book or magazine; any future use in other products would require a new fee to be negotiated with the illustrator. In advertising, it is more common to buy "all rights." Copyright in your work is assigned to the client, who then has unlimited exclusive use.

As media owners take advantage of the Internet to repurpose their products, even editorial clients are likely to ask for all rights. Find out the usual terms for your local market, and ask what the client expects before agreeing to a price.

If your work is reproduced in print, on the Internet, or anywhere else, by someone who has not licensed it, this is usually an infringement of your copyright. It does not matter where, how, or why the reproduction was made, how many people saw it, whether or not someone profited from it, or whether or not you were credited as the author of the work (though these factors could affect the exact outcome of a lawsuit). You can order the person responsible, or anyone involved in the reproduction and distribution of the work—such as a printer, Internet service provider, or bookseller—to desist, and demand appropriate compensation.

By the same token, if you take artistic material from any source—for example, by scanning or downloading it—and incorporate it into your work, this is likely to infringe somebody else's rights.

Many digital illustrators use "found" imagery as part of their style of work, and there are two legal ways of doing so. The first is to obtain permission from the copyright holder. The second is to use work that is explicitly released from copyright—for example, books and CD ROMs of "clip art," or books whose author has been dead for more than 70 years, so that copyright has expired. It is often assumed that unauthorized use is acceptable if the source is disguised, perhaps by using only fragments of the material or heavily manipulating it. But this does not avoid infringement, it only reduces your likelihood of getting caught. A number of digital illustrators have failed to get away with it, including mapmakers who have traced over existing maps and illustrators who have created homages to 20th-century artists. If your work is going to be published, it is best not to take any risks.

Image libraries offer an accessible source of properly licensed material. Rights-managed libraries charge different prices according to the intended use of the image; this is rarely suitable for illustrators because use of your finished work will be limited by the same terms. Royalty-free libraries charge a fixed price per image for unlimited use. On the Internet, you can search each catalog yourself (rather than paying the owner to do so, as in the past), then pay by credit card and download the images immediately. For single-use illustrations, this is an ideal solution. If, however, you need multiple pictures on a given theme for a larger project, royalty-free collections on CD ROMs will be significantly more cost effective.

Left: Rather than buying individual images, it is often worth investing in ready-made collections supplied on CD ROM. Each represents a particular style of material on a given theme, and offers a dozen or more pictures for the price of two or three.

Left: Specialist catalogs can be invaluable to the illustrator. Hemera Photo-Objects, at Ablestock.com, offers pictures of everyday items cleanly shot from a number of angles. These images are also available in large CD ROM albums.

# REFERENCE

**TECHNICAL REFERENCE**

7

**RESOLUTION** Before starting work on an illustration in bitmap software such as Adobe Photoshop, it's essential to know how the final artwork will be reproduced and at what size. From this you can calculate the necessary pixel size of the image, which is set when you first create your document.

Images destined for the web, to be viewed on computer monitors, are commissioned to a pixel size, such as 470 x 60 pixels, for an advertising banner. To maintain finer control over your material, you may wish to work at a higher resolution—perhaps double this size—before reducing the finished piece to the required dimensions.

Print work demands much higher resolutions. In CMYK output, color images are made up from dots of the four ink colors by a process called halftoning. Depending on the mechanical equipment used, output resolution may be determined by the press itself, if digital; the platesetter, which creates printing plates from digital artwork; or the imagesetter, which outputs color-separated films from which plates are manufactured. The native resolution of this

Below left: The table shows the size at which two images of different pixel dimensions would appear on the monitor, and the maximum size at which they could properly be printed. Note the dramatic difference between the two—an image may look huge when viewed at 100% in software, but that doesn't mean it can be output at a large size. For a rough idea of printable size, view images at 25% magnification. We have also shown the image size in megapixels, often used to describe the resolution offered by digital cameras. This figure is obtained by multiplying the linear pixel dimensions to give the area, then dividing by 1 million. You can see that 6 megapixels—quite a respectable digital camera specification—is still barely enough to fill a magazine page, even without cropping.

| Resolution and Print size guide | | |
|---|---|---|
| Number of pixels | 800 x 600 | 3000 x 2000 |
| Digital camera resolution | 0.5 megapixel | 6 megapixel |
| IMPERIAL | | |
| Nominal monitor size (72 ppi) | 11 1/8 x 8 1/3" | 41 2/3 x 27 3/4" |
| Maximum print size (300 ppi) | 2 2/3 x 2" | 10 x 6 2/3" |
| METRIC | | |
| Nominal monitor size (72 ppi) | 282 x 212mm | 1058 x 706mm |
| Maximum print size (300 ppi) | 68 x 51mm | 254 x 169mm |

Monochrome line art is a special case for print resolution. Because a black line is printed using only black ink, no halftoning is performed, and artwork pixels translate directly into hard-edged areas of black ink. Without the slight blurring of a halftone screen, pixels may be visible as tiny steps even at 300ppi. To show this, the artwork has been vector drawn. Printed from the original vector file (below),

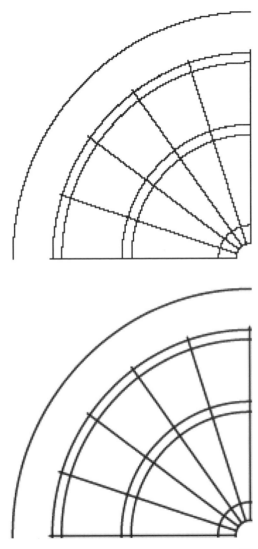

the lines are rasterized by the imagesetter at its full native resolution of around 2500ppi, and appear completely smooth. If we store the artwork as a 300ppi bitmap, output (top right) is not as clean. Line art that has to be reproduced in bitmap form should ideally be saved at 1200ppi or higher, but anti-aliasing can give smooth results, albeit not as sharp, at 300ppi (right).

# Resolution

device determines the number of dots of each ink that can be printed per linear inch, usually around 2,500.

To produce any given color, however, multiple dots of different inks must be combined, and this means the smallest area that can be resolved—the printed equivalent of a pixel—is much larger than a single ink dot. This is called the screen ruling, and is measured in lines per inch (lpi). Commonly used screens in high quality color printing, as in magazines and books, are 133lpi and 150lpi. For optimum results, the image to be output should be of a higher resolution than the screen ruling, but no benefit will be seen beyond about twice this value. Hence the figure of 300 pixels per inch that's used as a general guide for printed material. (Newspapers may use a coarser screen, requiring fewer pixels.)

We have correctly described image resolution in pixels per inch (ppi), but dots per inch (dpi) is often loosely used to refer to resolution regardless of context. You'll frequently see dpi used in reference to bitmap image resolution, just remember that when referring to pixels this is really ppi. Physical dimensions must be given along with this figure to determine the number of pixels, which will be equal to the printed size (in inches) multiplied by the resolution.

The use of pixel dimensions for on-screen work makes monitor resolution irrelevant, but for the sake of argument it's traditionally given as 72dpi, even though actual display resolutions are typically higher and vary from one manufac-

turer's model to the next.. So "72dpi" is used as a shorthand term for images sized for on-screen viewing. It's also used by print production staff to refer to any image mistakenly supplied at low resolution, and thus unsuitable for printing at the intended size.

You can change the resolution of an image at any time by entering new dimensions. This is known as resampling. In Photoshop, it's done via the Image Size command. A process of interpolation is used by the software to build a smaller or larger number of pixels from the existing data. This is very effective when reducing sizes, although you may need to apply a little sharpening afterward. Enlarging is much less satisfactory, as the software is being asked to invent data that doesn't exist within the picture, and a degree of fuzziness is unavoidable. Working at the correct resolution, or higher, is the only way to produce clean, sharp images.

Vector drawings have no inherent resolution, since they consist of scalable geometric descriptions. Even so, resolution issues can arise in drawing programs. When you blend between two objects to create a graduation between colors, for example, the number of steps in the blend should be set according to the intended output size of the artwork. The exact figure is hard to determine, as it depends on the degree of tonal variation, but you should allow at least 24 steps per inch. Resolution is also an issue when advanced vector effects, such as soft glows and shadows, have to be rasterized for output.

At 300dpi, this image—500 x 500 pixels— appears a little smaller than two inches square. Its size could be increased a little beyond this without visibly compromising quality, but not too far.

72dpi reproduction may look fine on the monitor, but it would be unacceptable in print. At first glance, the image looks wrong. On closer inspection the square pixels are all too visible.

When an image is halftoned, the extra resolution of the printing process is used to place many dots of different inks within each pixel of the image, enabling the full color gamut to be reproduced.

| Image Size | | |
| --- | --- | --- |
| Pixel Dimensions: 74K (was 174K) | | |
| Width: | 504 | pixels |
| Height: | 504 | pixels |
| Document Size: | | |
| Width: | 1.68 | inches |
| Height: | 1.68 | inches |
| Resolution: | 300 | pixels/inch |
| ☑ Constrain Proportions | | |
| ☑ Resample Image: Bicubic | | |

| Image Size | | |
| --- | --- | --- |
| Pixel Dimensions: 174K | | |
| Width: | 244 | pixels |
| Height: | 244 | pixels |
| Document Size: | | |
| Width: | 0.813 | inches |
| Height: | 0.813 | inches |
| Resolution: | 300 | pixels/inch |
| ☑ Constrain Proportions | | |
| ☐ Resample Image: Bicubic | | |

In Photoshop's Image Size dialog box (left), we can see the reduced width and height of the cropped image. If we re-enter the original dimensions and select Resample with Bicubic interpolation, Photoshop will recreate the cropped image with the original number of pixels. Because the missing pixels have been artificially generated, the result is not completely smooth and sharp.

This image, as it stands, contains sufficient pixels to create a density of 300 dots per inch when reproduced at its current size. Cropping the image down to a small portion

of the original area reduces the number of pixels. If we use the cropped image to fill the same space, the enlarged pixels become visible.

**COLOR MODES** It can often be a source of frustration to illustrators that they create bright, vibrant colors on-screen, but these colors turn out dull and flat when the work is printed on paper. This is not a fault with their printer or their bureau—it is inherent in the way color works.

# Color Modes

Computer screens and printing inks create colors in precisely opposite ways. Monitors, like televisions, use light to create color; the more colors you add, the brighter the result. This is known as "additive" color, so if you add all the colors together at full strength, you get white. The colors used are Red, Green, and Blue, so the color model employed by monitors is known as RGB.

With printing ink, however, the more color you add, the darker the result. This is known as "subtractive" color, so if you add all the colors together, you get black—actually, you get a rather murky brown, which is why the standard Cyan, Magenta, and Yellow printing colors are joined by Black to give depth. This color model is known as CMYK—where K stands for "Key" ("B" for Black would cause confusion with Blue).

The problem is that users want to see on-screen an accurate representation of how their color will look when it is printed. Using a complex conversion process, design programs simulate printed colors fairly well—but few of them limit you to just the range of colors that are printable. Your computer will also let you create dazzling greens, fluorescent pinks and startling blues—all of which are easily created using red, green, and blue lights, but which are simply impossible using CMYK inks.

Above: The cyan, magenta, yellow, and black plates in a printed CMYK image make up the color picture. Note how the red quadrant on the shirt is composed of solid magenta and yellow, with just the barest touch of cyan and black.

Left: The red, green, and blue channels in an RGB image make up the full-color final image. Here, light areas add to the color and dark areas are neutral, so the red quadrant on the shirt shows up as black on the green and blue channels, since no light is added in those areas. The white background is made up of solid red, solid green, and solid blue.

# Color Modes

Right: Printed colors use cyan, magenta, and yellow inks to create the different hues; black ink is added only to create depth in the shadow areas.

The problem also arises when scanning color photographs. All scanners, like all monitors, work in RGB, but it is up to the user to recognize the colors that are "out of gamut" (that is, unprintable using CMYK), and to de-saturate or change them. When working in Photoshop, it is a frequent occurrence to see your work suddenly look dull when you change its mode from RGB to CMYK—

this is not a shortcoming of Photoshop, but an attempt to show you how your work will look when printed. Fortunately, Photoshop employs a special CMYK Preview mode, which simulates the way colors will look when printed, thus letting you to make adjustments as appropriate.

The lack of scope of CMYK printing inks (also known as "process colors") is particularly appar-

Right: Computer monitors create color by adding red, green, and blue lights to a black screen. The more color is added, the brighter the result.

ent when you compare, say, a painting in a gallery to its printed version in a book or on a postcard. Process color printing may enable a CMYK printer to approximate a wide range of color, but it is just an approximation—and there are times when the comparison falls far short.

A point of interest is the overlap that occurs when colors are mixed. Red and green lights create yellow; blue and green create cyan; and red and blue create magenta. The opposite is true of CMYK colors: magenta and yellow make red; cyan and yellow make green; and, magenta and cyan make blue. As the examples on this page show, the RGB and CMYK models are almost diametrically opposed color systems, the former "additive," the latter "subtractive."

**FAR FROM BEING** incapable of error, computers just make mistakes more predictably than the rest of us. Nowhere is this truer than in the digital representation of color. It is easy to create any color you like in software, but that does not mean that what you see on your monitor will be precisely reproduced on anyone else's, let alone in print.

# Color Management

Each program has its own way of handling color, and every digital device is susceptible to its own inaccuracies. Color management attempts to compensate for these differences and match colors as precisely as possible

The International Color Consortium is an industry body established to research color technology and maintain internationally agreed standards. Central to its efforts is the principle of color space translation. On the previous page, we saw how the RGB system used for monitor display differs from CMYK printing. In fact, there are many and various RGB and CMYK models, in addition to several completely different ways of

## Determine your display's native response

This is the first of five steps used to determine the display's native luminance response curves.

Move the left slider until the brightness of the grey shape in the middle matches the backgrounds as much as possible. Move the right slider until the shape is neutral compared to its background. It may help to squint or sit back from the display.

After you have done this step, click the Continue button.

( Go Back )   ( Continue )

Left: Hardware calibration and profiling devices are best, but here we are using Apple's Display Calibrator Assistant in Expert Mode. This walks the user through a series of steps to establish the right ColorSync profile. This is accessed from the Display controls in the Mac's System Preferences.

### Determine your display's current gamma

Your display's actual gamma is affected by contrast and brightness settings and other characteristics of your display.

For each of the three colors below, move the slider until the shape in the middle blends in with the background as much as possible. It may help to squint or step back from the display.

Native Gamma = 2.47, 2.59, 2.20

After you have done this step, click the right arrow.

### Select a target gamma

Select your desired gamma setting for this display. This will adjust the overall contrast of the display. Watch the picture on the right to see the effect of the different options. In most cases, it is best to use the Mac Standard gamma of 2.2.2

Linear — Standard

1.0    1.8    2.2

☐ Use native gamma

Target Gamma = 2.20

After you have done this step, click the Continue button.

Top left: The sliders help determine the display's native luminance response. Sit back and squint as you slide the controls around until the apple is hard to see. There are five different brightness levels to work through.

Top right: Gamma refers to the position of the midpoint between white and black and how the display is driven to reproduce this. Changing this value biases the display toward lighter or darker tones. The monitor's existing gamma is determined by moving the

slider. Macs used to default to a gamma of 1.8, which matches print, while PCs used 2.2 instead. Both now use a gamma of 2.2 by default. Using a lower gamma will render midtones lighter.

Below left: Color temperature refers to an overall bias toward blue, at the "cold" end of the scale, or red, at the "hot" end. Changing the white point has an effect similar to viewing materials under different lighting. Most monitors are now set to very cold (high)

values, but a warmer setting will better reflect the appearance of typical daylight viewing conditions.

Below right: Once named, a summary of the changes is shown. You can then switch between different profiles as you wish. Making profiles this way is simple, but we do recommend considering a hardware calibration device for professional-level color accuracy.

### Select a target white point

Select the white point setting you want for your display. This will adjust the overall color tint of the display. In most cases it is best to use the display's native white point or a standard white point such as D50 or D65.

D50    D65    9300

5000 6000 7000 8000 9000

☑ Use native white point

Target White = 6507 °K

After you have done this step, click the Continue button.

### Conclusion

A new calibrated display profile has been created and set to be the current profile for this display.

You can change the current profile for this display bu using the Displays pane of System Preferences or the Devices pane of ColorSync Utility.

Profile Summary:

| | | |
|---|---|---|
| Name: | Color LCD Hand–calibrated | |
| Native Gamma: | 1.95, approximate | |
| Target Gamma: | 2.20 | |
| **Chromaticities** | **x** | **y** |
| Red Phosphor: | 0.641 | 0.339 |
| Green Phosphor: | 0.334 | 0.641 |
| Blue Phosphor: | 0.145 | 0.054 |
| Native White Point: | 0.313 | 0.329  6507 °K, approximate |
| Target White Point: | Native | |

To quit the calibrator, click the Done Button.

# Color Management

representing color. The ICC has chosen a model known as CIE-Lab as its fundamental "connection space."

Because its gamut is wide enough to encompass most RGB and CMYK spaces, the color values used by almost any device can be accurately translated into CIE-Lab, as long as the software that makes the translation is given specific information about that device. This information is provided in a standard form known as an input profile. Similarly, CIE-Lab color values can be translated into those of any device using an output profile.

Once you have profiles for all your equipment, it is theoretically possible to maintain accurate color. Images captured by a scanner or digital camera are translated via the color management system into the working space of your software. While you work, image data remains stored in this form, but is displayed on-screen translated into the RGB space of your monitor. If you print proofs of your work, colors are translated into the printer's CMYK color space. When clients receive your work and check it on-screen, it is translated into the working space of their software, and into the RGB space of their moni-

Right: The very cold color temperatures commonly applied to monitors, such as 9300K (right), tend to make images appear bluish and slightly washed out. Warmer temperatures, such as the prepress standard D65 (opposite), provide a better simulation of printed output, but may look unnaturally yellow to eyes accustomed to on-screen settings.

tor. Finally, your artwork is translated into the CMYK color space of the printing press. The appearance of colors should remain the same throughout the process.

This is all very well in principle, but it depends on every device having an accurate ICC profile, and every piece of software being correctly set up. This is hard to achieve. Most imaging devices come with ICC profiles, but these are generic; they describe the characteristics of the hardware as designed, but not the vagaries of the individual unit. The only way to ensure precision is to create profiles calibrated to your own devices, and update them to account for any variation over time. This requires additional software and skills. You will also need to understand the color management facilities of your software in order to make settings that improve color conversion, rather than further confusing the matter.

In any case, even perfect color management cannot guarantee perfect results. Clients might take your carefully calibrated work and output it without any color management at all. If your work is destined for print, the limited gamut of CMYK output will always prevent certain colors appearing accurately. Work for on-screen viewing on the Internet is entirely dependent on the hardware and software used by viewers.

In practice, most illustrators are content to calibrate their monitor by eye, so that they can be reasonably confident of seeing colors correctly on screen, and to use the profiles supplied with any other imaging hardware they may use, such as scanners and color printers. ICC color management is supported on Macintosh computers by Apple's ColorSync, and on PCs running Windows by Microsoft's ICM. It is also implemented within most professional graphics programs.

**FILE FORMATS** One of the advantages of working digitally is that you can keep a lifetime's work, including early drafts and multiple versions, in a space smaller than a shoebox. It's still important, however, to think about exactly how you store it, and when you send work to clients you'll need to be sure it's in a form they can use.

# File formats

There are many different formats for bitmap, vector, 3D, and animation files. All of them can be categorized into three groups: native formats, transfer formats, and output formats. Native files store data specifically for the program you're using, often including a large amount of information beyond the artwork itself. When you save from Photoshop, for example, its PSD file format records all the layers, masks, channels, paths, and guides in the current document, so that everything is present and correct when you load it back in.

Few other programs would be able to understand all of these components, and they are not necessary for final output, so you would normally store and supply finished artwork in a simpler output format containing just the image data. If you needed to import your artwork into a different application with some non-image features kept intact, such as alpha channels, you could use a standard file type capable of storing limited non-image information in a widely readable form. That would be a transfer format.

Despite the steadily increasing storage capacities of computers and media, artwork files can still prove cumbersome. Vector files are the smallest, usually taking a few hundred kilobytes

**Comparison of common image file formats**

| FORMAT | BITMAP/VECTOR | COMPRESSION | FEATURES | | | SUITABILITY | | | |
|--------|---------------|-------------|----------|---|---|-------------|---|---|---|
| | VECTOR | | A | L | P | C | T | O | P |
| AI | Vector | n/a | N | Y | Y | Y | Y | N | X |
| EPS | Both | None | N | N | Y | Y | Y | N | Y |
| GIF | Bitmap | Lossy* | N | N | N | N | N | Y | N |
| JPEG | Bitmap | Lossy | N | N | Y | Y | N | Y | Y |
| PNG | Bitmap | Lossless | N | N | N | N | Y | Y | N |
| PSD | Bitmap | Lossless | Y | Y | Y | Y | X | N | N |
| TIFF | Bitmap | Lossless | Y | Y | Y | Y | Y | N | Y |

*GIF reduces color depth to 8 bit but is otherwise lossless

Key

Y = yes, N = no, X = sometimes

Key to features:

A = alpha channels, L = layers, P = paths, C = CMYK

Key to suitability:

T = transfer, W = on-screen output (e.g. web), P = printed output at most. A multilayered Photoshop bitmap of a full-page illustration, by contrast, can exceed 100 MB. Even if you have enough storage space to cope with such files, moving them around is a problem: a 100 MB file can take half an hour to upload using a broadband Internet connection, and virtually no email service would accept it as an attachment.

The solution is compression. Using various mathematical processes, the data contained in a bitmap can be represented more efficiently. For example, a series of identical pixels can be described by storing the color value just once, along with the number of instances. This is known as lossless compression, and is used by many native and transfer formats, including PSD and TIFF. Lossless compression can be used to save files that you may want to work on again, including backup copies for archive purposes, as long as your chosen file format can accommodate all the aspects of the document that you need to preserve for editing.

To generate even smaller files, more aggressive compression can be allowed to throw away data. Methods are designed to preserve pixel values that have the greatest impact on appearance, so that the amount discarded is disproportionate to the impact on image quality. Files can easily be reduced to a fifth of their size, and often more. This lossy compression is suitable only for output formats, since image quality degrades cumulatively if you repeatedly load and save files. While working it is safer to stick with TIFF or PSD. JPEG is the most popular lossy format, and offers a scale of quality levels.

Although vector files are more straightforward than bitmaps, there are fewer satisfactory non-native formats. EPS used to be the only reliable format for vector graphics, but PDF is a good and widely-supported option today. Adobe Illustrator's native file format (AI) is based on the PDF format.

With moving pictures, compression is almost unavoidable, since the amounts of data involved would be impractically large without it. Vector formats such as Flash neatly get around this, but bitmapped material will need to be compressed using one of various codecs (compressor/decompressors). These are usually asymmetrical, meaning more processing is involved in compression (which may take a long time), than in decompression, which in most cases happens in real time as the movie plays. Advanced compression techniques may require expensive software and additional hardware, but many good codecs are supplied with the most widely used video-editing programs. Your choice will depend on the delivery format, which should be specified by the client. A website, for example, might specify Apple QuickTime format encoded in h.264 at medium compression.

---

### File format pronunciation guide

Before discussing file formats with clients, you'll need to get both your head and your tongue around all the acronyms.

| Name | Stands for | Pronunciation |
|------|-----------|---------------|
| EPS | Encapsulated PostScript | "Ee-pee-ess" |
| GIF | Graphics interchange format | "giff"* |
| TIFF | Tagged image file format | "Tiff" |
| JPEG | Joint Photographic Experts Group | "Jay-peg" |
| MPEG | Moving Picture Experts Group | "Em-peg" |
| PNG | Portable network graphic | "Ping" |

*Officially "jiff" but rarely used

# File formats

Saved as an uncompressed TIFF, this full-quality image in standard 24-bit color occupies 844 K of disk space.

Using LZW compression within the TIFF format, file size is reduced to 536 K without any reduction in quality.

Saved in JPEG format at a quality rating of 10, close to the top of the scale, the image is reduced to 204 K without obvious degradation.

At a JPEG quality of 5, file size falls to 148 K, and blocky artifacts are starting to become visible around edges and in dark areas.

As a GIF, the image takes just 168 K, but this format's 8-bit color depth can't render subtle tonal changes, as in the red background.

Dithering the GIF (a sort of random halftone) smooths transitions, but is noticeable as speckling, and increases file size to 212 K.

At a quality of 0, this 116 K JPEG doesn't look as bad as you might expect, but would be unacceptable for publication.

**ADOBE PHOTOSHOP** comes with a huge range of "filters"—image modifications based on dialog boxes, which show a preview of the filtered image, together with a set of sliders that change the intensity and type of effect. Many of these filters are for specialized use, producing artistic and sometimes zany results. Some, however, will be needed on a more regular basis.

# Essential Photoshop Filters

The two main everyday filter sets are Sharpen and Blur. Sharpening is used to add contrast and definition to soft images—most scanned photographs can be improved with the judicious use of sharpening. Although there are simple Sharpen and Sharpen More filters, the best results are gained using the curiously named Unsharp Mask. This filter works by comparing each pixel to its neighbors, using parameter sliders to change the intensity of the sharpening process. Likewise, although there are Blur and Blur More filters, Gaussian Blur will give more controllable results. Other Blur filters include Motion Blur and Radial Blur; the latter can be set to produce either a spinning or zooming blur effect.

Blur filters are commonly used for removing unwanted noise—either the moiré pattern caused by scanning printed images, or the "blockiness" created when images, typically those captured by digital cameras, over-compress the results in order to fit them onto their storage medium. A variety of filters found under the Noise category can also assist in this task.

Opposite:

1. This is the original globe image, with no filters applied.

2. An application of the Unsharp Mask filter, used at 100% with a radius of 2 pixels. This setting is enough to bring out the detail in the globe, letting some of the text be more easily read.

3. With the Unsharp Mask filter set to 300% at a radius of 5 pixels, the effect is greatly exaggerated. Although this works well on some areas—the stand, for example, is now bright and shiny—the colors in the globe have become over-saturated, and the image is starting to look quite artificial.

4. Here, we have used the same settings as the previous example, but increased the Threshold setting from 0 to 40. This retains the sharpening where it is needed—making the text more legible—but lowers it on areas of flat color.

# Essential Photoshop Filters

1. Blur filters can be used to add life to static images. Here, we'll use a couple of Blur filters to make this sports car move. The car, incidentally, is on a different layer from the background, so the filter will only affect that element.

2. With Motion Blur applied, the whole car appears to be whizzing by too fast to see it clearly, but there is certainly a sense of movement captured there.

3. When the Motion Blur filter is applied to a duplicate of the car layer, we can use a Layer Mask to selectively hide parts of the blurred layer, letting the original car show through.

4. A final touch is to add Radial Blur to the front wheel, which previously looked too static. Now, it is spinning as fast as the car is moving.

1. This image is a typical example of those captured with digital cameras.

2. The blockiness (here exaggerated to show the effect) is created by JPEG compression of the original image.

3. Gaussian Blur, here used at a radius of 2 pixels, smoothes out the blocks, but the entire image now looks fuzzy.

4. The Median filter—also applied with a 2 pixel radius—does a similar job, but hard edges, such as the cap badge, remain sharp.

5. The Dust and Scratches filter is designed for removing marks from old photographs—but here, again with a radius of 2 pixels, it smoothes out the blockiness without smudging the edges.

# Artistic Filters

Dry Pencil creates the effect that the image has been drawn using loose pencil strokes on a gray background.

Fresco reproduces the effect of an image painted onto wet plaster.

Paint Daubs creates a roughly painted effect, using a variety of textures.

Plastic Wrap makes an object look like it is encased in polythene, and is useful for creating liquid and glass effects, too.

Sponge imposes a random, tight texture, as if the image has been painted with a natural sponge.

Poster Edges superimposes a degraded photocopy effect on the image, with added grain.

# Distortion Filters

Pinch pulls the image in toward the center, performing an effect opposite to that of Spherize.

Spherize makes an object look as if it has been photographed through a fish-eye lens. It is useful for making objects appear spherical—such as turning rock images into planets.

Zigzag applies rippled distortions to make an object appear as if multiple Twirl filters had been applied at different radii. It is useful for creating pond effects on water.

Twirl spins an object around, producing a stronger effect at the center than at the edges. Use it for making wheels appear as if in motion.

Glass makes an object look as if it has been photographed through a rippled glass window.

Polar Co-ordinates creates an object that would look like the original if viewed reflected in a cylindrical mirror placed at its center. It is useful for bending straight objects around curves.

# Pixellate Filters

Color Halftone simulates the effect of four-color printing. By setting all the colors to the same screen angle, an image can be converted to an array of regular dots.

Crystallize creates an array of random, single-color shapes from an image that follow the hues of the original.

Mezzotint simulates the effect produced by antique printing techniques, before halftone screens were invented.

Mosaic produces an exaggerated bitmap effect, as if a tiny object had been greatly enlarged. It is useful for simulating images viewed on screens.

Pointillize simulates the dot-painting technique pioneered by Seurat and the other Pointillist painters.

Fragment creates multiple superimposed copies of an image, as if the object had been shaken violently while being photographed.

# Sketch Filters

Bas Relief makes an object look as if it has been carved in stone on a flat surface.

Chalk & Charcoal makes an object seem to have been drawn with those materials. The foreground color is applied to dark areas, the background color to light areas, and those in between are filled in with a mid-tone gray.

Conté Crayon simulates drawing with crayons on a textured surface. Any grayscale image can be used for the background texture.

Notepaper creates a threshold effect, as if the object has been embossed onto textured paper.

Photocopy makes an object look as if a picture of it has been photocopied. The foreground color is the ink color, the background color the paper color.

Water paper simulates the effect of painting onto a textured, absorbent surface, as if the paint had run along the paper grain.

# Stylize Filters

Diffuse roughens the edges of objects, both internally and externally.

Emboss raises the outlines between light and dark areas in an object, as if they have been impressed onto paper and sharply lit from the side.

Extrude makes an object appear to be made of blocks or pyramids that radiate from the center. The height and number of blocks are both controllable.

Glowing Edges selects just the borders between light and dark areas, and makes them appear as if made of neon lighting.

Tiles makes an object appear as if made of irregularly placed tiles in a regular rectangular mosaic.

Wind streaks an object from left to right or right to left, producing a stylized blur effect.

# Texture Filters

Craquelure simulates the cracking effect seen on very old paintings.

Grain makes an object appear to have been printed on a distressed surface. A variety of grain types may be selected.

Mosaic Tiles gives the impression of the object having been constructed from irregularly damaged tiles, with darker grouting between the tiles.

Patchwork makes an object look as if it has been sewn in the style of a Victorian sampler.

Stained Glass breaks an object down as if it were made into a stained glass window, with leading between each pane.

Texturizer applies any grayscale image as a texture on an image, as if it has been lit from the side.

# Glossary

**4-bit** The allocation of four data bits to each pixel, giving an image or screen display of 16 grays or colors.

**8-bit** The allocation of eight data bits to each pixel, producing a display or image of 256 grays or colors.

**16-bit color** A facility in some image-editing applications, such as Photoshop, that allows you to work on images in 16-bit-per-channel mode rather than 8-bit mode. RGB (qv) images use three 8-bit channels (totalling 24 bits), while CMYK (qv) images use four 8-bit channels (totalling 32 bits). A 16-bit-per-channel image provides finer control over color, but the resulting file size is much larger.

**24-bit color** The allocation of 24 bits to each pixel, giving a screen display of 16.7 million colors.

**aliasing** The term describing the jagged appearance of bitmapped (qv) images or fonts as a result of insufficient resolution or excessive enlargement.

**alpha channel** A grayscale channel containing information regarding the transparency of pixels. In image files this is a separate channel—additional to the three RGB (qv) or four CMYK (qv) channels—where masks (qv) are stored.

**animated GIF** A GIF (qv) file containing more than one image. Many programs, including web browsers, will display each of the images in turn, thus producing an animation. The only file format for animated sequences that does not depend on the presence of a browser plug-in for playback on web pages.

**animation** The process of creating a moving image by rapidly moving from one still image to the next.

**antialiasing** A technique for eliminating the jagged effect of bitmapped (qv) images or text reproduced on low-resolution devices such as monitors. This is achieved by adding pixels of an in-between tone, blending the rough edges of the object's color with those of the background.

**artifact** A visible flaw in an electronically prepared image, usually occurring as a result of the imaging technique employed.

**artwork** Any drawings, paintings, photographs or other graphic materials—in either physical or digital media—that are prepared for use in an animation.

**background** The area of an image on which the principal foreground subject sits.

**bevel** A chamfered edge applied to type, buttons, or selections as a 3D effect.

**Bézier curve** A curve whose shape is defined by a pair of "direction lines" at each end. These specify the direction and rate at which the curve leaves or enters the corresponding end point. By manipulating the lines you can change the shape of the curve.

**bit** A contraction of binary digit. The smallest piece of information a computer can use. Expressed as one of two values: 1 or 0.

**bit depth** The number of bits assigned to each pixel on a display or in an image, affecting the range of colors that can be reproduced.

**bitmap** An image formed from a matrix of pixels, each with its own specific color value.

**bump map** A bitmap image file, normally grayscale (qv), which is

most frequently used in 3D applications for modifying surfaces or applying textures. The gray values in the image are assigned height values, with black representing the troughs and white the peaks.

**byte** A single group made up of eight individual bits (0s and 1s) of data, which can be processed together as one unit.

**CAD** Abbreviation for "computer-aided design." Strictly speaking, any design carried out using a computer, but generally used with reference to 3D technical design.

**calibration** The process of adjusting a piece of hardware to conform to a known scale or standard so that it performs more accurately.

**capture** The action of getting an image in digital form by taking a photograph, scanning an image into a computer, or "grabbing" an image using a frame grabber.

**clip art / clip media** Collections of (usually) royalty-free photographs, illustrations, design devices and other multimedia objects—including movies, sounds, and 3D wireframes—that are designed to be used in other projects.

**clipping** Limiting an image or any part of an image to the bounds of a particular area.

**clipping path** A Bézier (qv) outline that defines which area of an image should be considered transparent or "clipped." This lets you isolate the foreground object and is particularly useful when images are to be placed over new backgrounds.

**CMYK** Abbreviation for "cyan, magenta, yellow, and black." The four printing-process colors based on the subtractive color model (black is represented by the letter K, standing for key plate). In color reproduction most of the colors are created from cyan, magenta, and yellow; the theory being that when all three are combined, they produce black. However, this is rarely achievable and usually undesirable—true black ink produces better results, too much CMY ink would be used, and drying times would be increased.

**collage** An image assembled from elements drawn from different sources. Originally used to describe those pieces produced by pasting together images culled from magazines (say) or fabric swatches. It now also describes images built in digital image-editing software, where the disparate origins of the separate components remain obvious. Also known as a montage or (in the case of photographic subjects) a photomontage.

**color correction** The process of adjusting color values during the reproduction process in order to achieve a desired result.

**color depth** Like bit depth (qv), the number of bits required to define the color of each pixel.

**color-management system** A method devised to provide accuracy and consistency of color representation across all devices in the color-reproduction chain.

**color picker (1)** A color model displayed on a computer monitor. Color pickers may be specific to an application (such as Adobe Photoshop), a third-party color model (such as PANTONE®), or to the operating system.

**color picker (2)** A book of printed color samples, carefully defined and graded, from which you can select spot colors. Color pickers generally

conform to a color model, such as PANTONE® (qv), so you can be confident that the color chosen will be faithfully reproduced when printed later on.

**color temperature** A measure of the composition of light. This is defined as the temperature—measured in degrees Kelvin—to which a black object would need to be heated in order to produce a particular color of light. The temperature of direct sunlight is around 5,000 K and is considered the ideal viewing standard in the graphic arts.

**compression** The technique of rearranging data so that it either occupies less space on disk or transfers more rapidly between devices or across a network.

**constrain** A facility in some applications to contain one or more items within another. For example, in a page layout application, a picture box (the "constrained item") sits within another picture box (the "constraining box").

**continuous tone** An image that contains infinite shades between the lightest and darkest tones. Most commonly used in reference to conventional, film-based photography.

**contrast** The degree of difference between adjacent tones in an image (or computer monitor) from the lightest to the darkest. High contrast describes an image with light highlights and dark shadows but with few shades in between, whereas a low-contrast image is one with even tones and few dark areas or highlights.

**copyright** The right of a person who creates an original work to protect that work by controlling how and where it can be reproduced. Note that ownership of the work does not automatically signify ownership of

copyright or vice versa—copyright is only transferred if the creator of the work assigns it in writing.

**copyright free** A misnomer used to describe ready-made resources such as clip art. In fact, these resources are rarely, if ever, copyright free—in most cases only a license to use the material is granted by purchase. The correct description would normally be "royalty free:" material that you can use—under license—free from payment of further fees or royalties.

**crop** To trim or mask an image so that it fits a given area, or to discard unwanted portions of an image.

**cross-platform** The term applied to software that will work on more than one computer platform (Mac OS and Windows, for example).

**definition** The overall quality—or clarity—of an image, determined by the combined subjective effect of graininess (or resolution (qv) in a digital image) and sharpness.

**density** The darkness of tone or color in any image. In a photographic transparency this would refer to the amount of light that could pass through it, so determining the darkness of shadows and the saturation of color.

**density range** The maximum range of tones in an image, measured as the difference between the maximum and minimum densities (the darkest and lightest tones).

**desaturate** To reduce the strength or purity of color in an image, thus making it look grayer.

**descreening** The technique of removing a halftone dot pattern from an image to avoid an undesirable moiré (qv) pattern occurring when a new halftone screen is applied.

# Glossary

**digital image** Image converted to (or created in) the digital domain. Elements of the image are represented by pixels with discrete color and brightness values.

**digital photography** The process of capturing an image with a digital camera. The term can also refer to the manipulation of photographic images on a computer.

**dots per inch (dpi)** A unit of measurement used to represent the resolution (qv) of devices such as printers and imagesetters and also, erroneously, monitors and screen images, where the resolution should more properly be expressed in pixels per inch (ppi).

**drawing application** Software used to create graphics from complex arrangements of objects, which are themselves defined using vectors.

**drop shadow** A shadow projected onto the background behind an image or character in order to lift it off the surface.

**electronic media** General term to describe media that uses electronic means for the dissemination and delivery of information.

**EPS** Abbreviation for "encapsulated PostScript." A standard graphics file format used primarily for storing the object-orientated, vector graphics files generated by a drawing application such as Adobe Illustrator or FreeHand.

**export** A feature provided by many applications to allow you to save a file in a format so that it can be used by another application or on a different operating system.

**eyedropper tool** In some applications, a tool for gauging the color of adjacent pixels.

**fill** In graphics applications, the content, such as color, tone, or pattern, applied to the inside of a shape (including type characters).

**file format** The way a program arranges data so that it can be stored or displayed on a computer. File formats range from unique formats peculiar to a particular application, to standard formats recognized by many different software programs.

**filter** A component of an application that processes or converts data. In graphics applications, the term is employed to describe the features used for the application of special effects to images.

**final rendering** The final computer generation of an image, once you have finished editing or modeling, most commonly used to refer to the application of final surface textures, lighting, and effects to complete a 3D object, scene, or animation.

**Flash** Software owned by Adobe for the creation of vector graphics and animations for web presentations. Flash generates small files, which are quick to download and—being vector (qv)—are scalable to any dimension without an increase in the file size.

**fractal** Infinitely variable shapes often characterized by extreme irregularity and defined by complex but precisely defined mathematical expressions. Some Photoshop filters make extensive use of fractal mathematics and patterning, allowing users to make bold graphics from scratch using image elements to create the pattern.

**frame** A single still picture from a movie or animation. Also a single complete image from a TV picture.

**frame-rate** The speed at which the individual frames of an animation are substituted for one another— that is, the speed at which the animation is played. Usually specified in frames per second.

**gamma** A measure of contrast in a digital image, a photographic film or paper, or a processing technique.

**gamma correction** Modification of the midtones (qv) of an image by compressing or expanding the range, thus altering the contrast.

**GIF** Acronym for "graphics interchange format." One of the main bitmapped (qv) image formats used on the Internet. A 256-color format with two specifications, GIF87a and, more recently, GIF89a, the latter providing additional features such as transparent backgrounds. The GIF format uses a lossless (qv) compression technique, and thus does not squeeze files as much as the lossy (qv) JPEG format.

**Gouraud shading** A method of adding shading to a 3D graphic through the selective manipulation of colors and shades along the lines of certain vertices, which are then averaged across each polygon face. Faster than Phong shading (qv), but the results are not as realistic.

**graduation / gradation** A smooth, continuous transition from one color or tone to another.

**graphic** A general term describing any illustration or drawn design.

**gray** Any neutral tone in the range between black and white, with no added color.

**grayscale** The rendering of an image in a range of 256 levels of gray from white to black.

**highlight** To mark an item, such as a section of text, an icon, or a menu command, to indicate that it is selected or active.

**HSL** Abbreviation for hue, saturation, lightness: a color model based upon the light transmitted either in an image or in your monitor. Hue (qv) is the spectral color (the actual pigment color), saturation the intensity of the color pigment (without black or white added), and brightness represents the strength of luminance from light to dark (the amount of black or white present).

**hue** The pure spectral color that distinguishes a color from others. Red is a different hue from blue; and although light red and dark red will contain varying amounts of white or black, they both have the same basic hue.

**icon** A graphical representation of an object (such as a disk, file, folder, or tool) used to make identification and selection easier.

**image area** The area within a final graphic document in which a particular image or group of images will have to fit.

**image library** A source of original transparencies and pictures that can be used for virtually any purpose on payment of a fee. The sums vary according to usage.

**image size** A description of the dimensions of an image in terms of linear dimensions, resolution (qv), or digital file size.

**imaging device** A general term describing any dedicated piece of equipment that captures an image from an original, such as a scanner or camera, or generates an image from a previously captured original.

**import** To bring text, pictures, or other data into a document.

**indexed color** An image mode of a maximum of 256 colors that is used in some applications, such as Adobe Photoshop, to reduce the file size of RGB (qv) images so that they can be used in multimedia presentations or on web pages. This is achieved by matching the colors used in an image to an indexed table of colors ("a color look-up table," or CLUT). If a color in the image does not appear in the table, then the application selects the nearest color or simulates it by arranging the available colors in a pattern.

**interpolation** A computer calculation used to estimate unknown values that fall between known ones. One use of this process is to redefine pixels in bitmapped (qv) images after they have been modified in some way, for instance, when an image is resized (called "resampling") or rotated, or if color corrections have been made.

**inverse kinematics** A method of animating structures that form a chain of links, such as a human arm. The position of all the elements in the chain—for example, forearm, elbow, upper arm—are computed to fit the position of the final element—the hand.

**inverting** A feature of many applications whereby an image bitmap is reversed—so that, for example, the black pixels appear white and vice versa, making a negative image.

**JPEG, JPG** Acronym for "joint photographic experts group:" an ISO (International Standards Organization) group that defines compression (qv) standards for bitmapped (qv) color images. The abbreviated form gives name to the widely used file format (qv).

**layer** In some applications and web pages, a level to which you can consign an element of the design you are working on, enabling you to work on it independently of the rest of the image.

**keyframe** A single animation or movie frame (qv) in which information is stored as a reference, so that subsequent frames only store changes in the frame rather than storing the whole frame each time. This makes animation and movie files much smaller.

**keyline** A line drawing indicating the size and position of an illustration in a layout.

**landscape format** An image or page format in which the width is greater than the height. Also called "horizontal format."

**layout** A drawing that shows the general appearance of a design, indicating, for example, the position of text and illustrations.

**line weight** The thickness of a line or rule in an image.

**lossless compression** Methods of file compression (qv) in which no data is lost during the process, meaning that quality is maintained.

**lossy compression** Methods of file compression (qv) in which some data may be irretrievably lost during the process. This can result in a drop in quality or the appearance of digital artefacts in the image.

**LZW** Abbreviation for Lempel-Ziv-Welch: A widely supported lossless compression (qv) method for bitmapped (qv) images.

**mask** A selected portion of an image, blocked out to protect it from alteration during all or part of the image-editing process.

# Glossary

**midtone** The range of tonal values in an image, covering the area between the darkest and lightest but usually referring to those that appear halfway.

**moiré** An unintended pattern that occurs in halftone reproduction when two or more colors are printed and the dot screens are positioned at the wrong angles.

**monochrome** An image of varying tones reproduced in a single color. Not necessarily black and white.

**MPEG** Abbreviation for Moving Picture Experts Group, the organization in charge of the development of standards for the coded representation of digital audio and video. Established in 1988, the group produced MPEG-1, the standard on which video CD and MP3 are based; MPEG-2, the standard used for digital television and DVD; and MPEG-4, the standard for multimedia (qv) on the web.

**multimedia** Any combination of digital media, such as sound, video, animation, graphics, and text, incorporated into a software product or presentation.

**online** Any activity that takes place on a computer or device while it is connected to a network, including the Internet.

**orientation** The print direction of a page, or format of an image (portrait or landscape).

**painting applications** Applications that use bitmaps (qv) to create images rather than vectors (qv).

**PANTONE®** The registered trademark of Pantone Inc.'s system of color standards and control and quality requirements, in which each color bears a description of its formulation (in percentages) for subsequent printing.

**perspective** A technique of rendering 3D objects on a 2D plane, duplicating the "real world" view by giving an impression of the object's relative position and size when viewed from a particular point.

**Phong shading** A superior but time-consuming method of rendering 3D images that computes the shading of every pixel. Usually reserved for the final rendering(qv).

**pixel** Abbreviation for picture element. The smallest component of any digitally generated image, including text. A single dot of light on a screen.

**pixel depth** The number of shades that a single pixel can display, determined by the number of bits used to display the pixel.

**pixelation / pixelization** The term used to describe an image that has been broken up into square blocks resembling pixels, giving it a "digitized" look.

**plug-in** Software, usually developed by a third party, that extends the capabilities of another piece of software. Plug-ins are common in image-editing and page-layout applications, providing specialized tools or unique effect filters.

**PNG** Abbreviation for "portable network graphics." A file format for images used on the web that provides 10–30% lossless compression, and supports variable transparency through alpha channels, cross-platform control of image brightness, and interlacing.

**portrait format** An image or page in a vertical format.

**posterize/posterization** To divide, by photographic or digital means, a continuous-tone image into a predefined or arbitrary number of flat tones.

**PostScript** Page-description language. PostScript code tells an output device how to construct a page from various text and graphic elements.

**primary colors** The pure colors from which—theoretically—all other colors can be mixed. In printing, they are the "subtractive" pigment primaries (cyan, magenta, and yellow). The primary colors of light, or "additive" primaries, are red, green, and blue.

**QuickTime** Apple's software program and system extension that enables computers running either Windows or the Mac OS to play movie and sound files, particularly over the Internet and in multimedia applications.

**raster image** An image defined as rows of pixels or dots.

**rasterize** The conversion of a vector graphics image into a bitmap. This may introduce aliasing, but is often necessary when preparing images for the web.

**raytracing** A rendering algorithm that simulates the physical and optical properties of light rays as they reflect off a 3D model, thus producing realistic shadows and reflections.

**real-time** The actual time in which things happen; on your computer, therefore, an event that corresponds to reality.

**rendering** The process of transforming raw image data and a set of program instructions into a new image or animation. In 3D applications, the term refers to wrapping a surface texture over a 3D body created as a "wire frame" in order to create realistic landscapes or turn wire-frame figures into characters. The wrapping is usually combined with other effects (such as lighting effects) to increase the realism.

**rescale** Amending the size of an image by proportionally reducing its height and width.

**resolution** The degree of quality, definition, or clarity with which an image is reproduced or displayed, for example in a photograph, or via a scanner, monitor screen, printer, or other output device.

**retouching** Altering an image, artwork, or film to modify or remove imperfections. Can be done using mechanical methods (knives, inks, and dyes) or digitally, using Photoshop and similar packages.

**RGB** Abbreviation for "red, green, blue." The primary colors of the additive color model—used in video technology (including computer monitors) and also for graphics that will not be printed by the four-color (CMYK) process. Web graphics are one example.

**rough** A preliminary drawing showing a proposed design. Also called a "scamp" or "visual."

**scanning** An electronic process that converts a hard copy of an image into digital form by sequential exposure to a moving light beam such as a laser.

**shading** In 3D applications, the resulting color of a surface due to light striking it at an angle.

**shadow areas** The areas of an image that are darkest or densest.

**shareware** Software available through user groups, magazine cover disks, etc., which is usually only paid for by those users who decide to continue using it. Shareware should not be

confused with Freeware, which is free to use for an unlimited period of time.

**sharpening** Enhancing the apparent sharpness of an image by increasing the contrast between adjacent pixels.

**smoothing** The refinement of bitmapped (qv) images and text by antialiasing (qv). Smoothing is also used in some drawing applications, where it is applied to a path to smooth a line, and in 3D modeling applications, where it is applied to the individual polygons to tweak resolution in the final rendering.

**thumbnail** A smaller representation of an image used for selection or identification purposes.

**TIFF**, TIF Abbreviation for "tagged image file format." A standard graphics file format (qv) originally developed by Aldus (now merged with Adobe) and Microsoft. Used for scanned, high-resolution, bitmapped (qv) images and for color separations.

**tiling** The repetition of a graphic item, with the repetitions placed side-by-side in all directions so that they form a pattern—just like tiles.

**tint** The resulting shade when white is added to a solid color.

**transparent GIF** A feature of the GIF89a file format that allows you to place a non-rectangular image directly on the background color of a web page.

**transpose / transposition** To exchange the position of any two images, either by design or because they are in the wrong order. For example, image layers may be transposed when a lower layer and higher one are positionally reversed. Animation cells can be transposed in a similar way.

**tweening** A contraction of "in-between." An animator's term for the process of creating transitional frames to fill in between key frames (qv) in an animation.

**unsharp masking** (USM) A traditional film-compositing technique used to sharpen an image. Some image-editing applications feature filters that replicate the effect.

**vector** A mathematical description of a line that is defined in terms of physical dimensions and direction. Vectors are used in drawing packages to define shapes (vector graphics) that can be repositioned or resized at will.

# Index

# Index

REFERENCE

# Index

# Index